MAKE A DIFFERENCE

The Founder of the I Have a Future Program
Shares His Vision for Young America

HENRY W. FOSTER, JR., M.D.,

WITH ALICE GREENWOOD

SCRIBNER

SCRIBNER
1230 Avenue of the Americas
New York, NY 10020

SCRIBNER and design are registered trademarks of Simon & Schuster Inc.

DESIGNED BY ERICH HOBBING

Text set in Garamond No. 3

Manufactured in the United States of America

1   3   5   7   9   10   8   6   4   2

Library of Congress Cataloging-in-Publication Data
Foster, Henry W., 1933–
Make a difference/Henry W. Foster with Alice Greenwood.
p. cm.
1. Foster, Henry W., 1933– . 2. Afro-American physicians—Biography.
I. Greenwood, Alice. II. Title.
R154.F714A3   1997
610'.92—dc21   96–48006
[B]   CIP

ISBN 0-684-82685-2

*This book is dedicated
to those who mean the most to me—
St. Clair, Myrna, Wendell, Ann,
and Claire Elizabeth.*

Contents

Foreword

Throughout my career in the United States Senate, the cause of quality health care for all Americans has been one of my primary concerns. The Committee on Labor and Human Resources, on which I serve, has the lead responsibility in the United States Senate for laws that affect public health—and one of its most important responsibilities is to review the qualifications of the individual nominated to be the Surgeon General of the United States—"the nation's doctor." The Surgeon General has a unique opportunity to shape public policy—and influence public opinion—on critical public health issues. C. Everett Koop's leadership in helping the nation respond constructively to the AIDS epidemic and Luther L. Terry's crusade to alert the nation to the health dangers of smoking made them two of the best-known Surgeon Generals who played a central role in changing American health care for the better.

I first came to know Henry Foster in 1995, when President Bill Clinton nominated him to be our country's physician in chief. The dramatic story of his remarkable life, his brilliant career, and his unsuccessful battle for confirmation by the Republican-controlled Senate is well told in this book. I was convinced then and I am even more convinced today that the failure to confirm Dr. Foster was an embarrassment for the Senate and a major lost opportunity for the nation.

Henry Foster's life is a story of great achievement. In a sense, he has been a pioneer all his life. In the course of his career, he has met and mastered many difficult challenges in medicine and in the larger world. He has had a positive effect in every community and every environment he has served. His life is both inspiring and fascinating. Throughout, he always took on the toughest challenges—and he was usually successful.

Henry Foster was born in 1933 in Pine Bluff, Arkansas. The son of two teachers, he learned to value education, and the opportunities it offered, early in life. He earned his undergraduate degree from Morehouse College in Atlanta in 1954, and was accepted by the University of Arkansas Medical School in Little Rock at the age of twenty—the only African-American in his class.

He decided to begin his practice of medicine in the rural South. At that time, relatively few doctors were willing to set up practice in disadvantaged areas. Young, able, well trained in modern medicine, and with a heart as big as his mind, Dr. Foster went to Tuskegee University, formerly the Tuskegee Institute, to work among the poor in racially divided rural Alabama. He practiced there for eight years, won renown for his ability, and returned to Nashville in 1973 as chairman of the department of obstetrics and gynecology at Meharry Medical College.

During his years in Tuskegee, the main local hospital served only whites, except for the occasional black emergency patients, who would be put in rooms normally used as closets. Most black patients went to the "other" hospital in Tuskegee, the John A. Andrew Hospital, where Dr. Foster was on duty—and saw to it that they received good care. In those years, Tuskegee suffered from a severe shortage of doctors, and Dr. Foster filled an urgent need. Most of his patients were poor, black women who had never seen a doctor in their entire lives before being treated by Dr. Foster. Most of them lived without electricity, without telephones, and, in many cases, without running water.

Most often these women had to have their babies at home, assisted if possible by midwives. Access to prenatal care was almost nonexistent. Dr. Foster provided it, often in life or death situations and under the most difficult circumstances.

These conditions would have been daunting to even the most seasoned physician. But Henry Foster was up to the challenge. He took sole responsibility for patients from five counties, with a caseload well into the hundreds. Perhaps his Air Force training had prepared him well for these near-battlefield conditions. He dedicated himself to providing the best health care he could—sometimes delivering as many as eight babies a day. The community remembers him as the town's revered "Baby Doctor," and in his thirty-eight-year career he has brought literally thousands of babies into the world.

As his practice and experience grew, Dr. Foster saw firsthand how the lack of adequate health care contributed to an inordinately high level of infant mortality in the region. He shifted to a higher gear, realizing that he had the background and commitment to master not only medical challenges but public health challenges as well. He applied for a grant from the Alabama Department of Health to expand the Maternal and Infant Care Program at Tuskegee Institute. He directed this program from 1970 to 1973, and had a significant impact in reducing infant mortality and giving children a healthy start in life. He brought together teams of doctors and other health-care specialists to provide a comprehensive range of health and social services to women and children in these rural communities. They reached out to women early in their pregnancies and identified those with potential complications so that they could receive proper health care throughout their pregnancies and following birth.

In his comprehensive approach to maternal and child care, Dr. Foster was well ahead of his time—so much so that his Tuskegee program became a national model for what is now known as "regionalized perinatal care," involving extensive community outreach, specialized services for high-risk women, and good pre- and postnatal care for mothers and infants. As a result of his accomplishments, Henry Foster became one of the nation's leading experts on maternal and child health.

His initiatives helped Alabama's poor to learn how to take better care of themselves and their infants. He began working with the Robert Wood Johnson Foundation to extend his health-care model to other parts of the country. In 1972, primarily because of his landmark work in this field, he received the high honor of being elected to the nation's prestigious Institute of Medicine. In 1978, he was appointed by Joseph Califano, President Jimmy Carter's Secretary of Health, Education and Welfare, to that cabinet department's Ethics Advisory Board, which had been created to examine the broad range of moral and ethical questions being raised by medical science.

In the 1970s, Dr. Foster had also begun a crusade to provide similar quality health care to adolescents. He was chosen by the Johnson Foundation to direct a multimillion-dollar grant program to increase health services for teenagers and young men and women. He concentrated on those between the ages of fifteen and twenty-four living in areas with high rates of teenage pregnancy, violence, drug and alcohol abuse, and mental illness. Under his guidance, twenty teaching hospitals across the country developed comprehensive health programs to expand services for youths and to train doctors and other health-care professionals in the specialized care of high-risk youth.

Between 1982 and 1986, as a result of Dr. Foster's initiative, these unique programs provided health services to 306,000 youths, and significantly increased the number of medical and other professionals trained in providing health care to adolescents.

Many of the nations first school-based health clinics were a direct result of this initiative. It was during this period that Dr. Foster began to develop a strategy for combating one of the most serious dangers to health and opportunity for adolescents in America— teenage pregnancy—which has become a crisis of significant proportions in all parts of the country. More than a million teenagers become pregnant each year. For every thousand women between the ages of fifteen and nineteen, 111 become pregnant in a year, the highest rate of teenage pregnancy in the industrial world.

As chairman of obstetrics and gynecology at Meharry, Dr. Foster had been training doctors to understand and appreciate the issues and attitudes of their patients, and to identify and work to overcome barriers to quality health services. His battle against teenage pregnancy was a logical outgrowth of those principles. Beginning in 1987, he went into the community, working closely with parents and community leaders in Nashville, to find solutions. He listened to teenagers themselves, and asked them what they needed to enable them to do better in school, stay out of trouble, and avoid pregnancy.

The result was Dr. Foster's nationally famous I Have a Future program. Since school-based clinics are not available when schools are closed, he developed a program to reach teenagers where they live, during the times when they need help the most—after school, on weekends, and especially during summers when they have the most free time and are at the greatest risk of getting into trouble.

The I Have a Future program targeted teenagers in two public housing developments in Nashville. Its goal is to reduce teenage pregnancy, while also addressing other serious problems facing inner-city youth such as drugs and alcohol abuse, crime and violence, unemployment, and lack of educational opportunity. The program raises participants' self-esteem, promotes abstinence from sex, and offers positive options to help teenagers stay in school, go on to college, and find the Up escalator to the American Dream.

Dr. Foster's vision and personal involvement made I Have a Future a model for the nation. The program won the initial financial support of prestigious national and local organizations, including the Carnegie Corporation and the W. T. Grant Foundation, and individuals such as Bill and Camille Cosby. The American Medical Association's National Congress for Adolescent Health honored the program for its success in preventing teenage pregnancy.

For more than two decades, Dr. Foster has trained thousands of America's finest medical practitioners, especially those who serve on the front lines. He has devoted his life and career to improving the health of mothers and infants, reducing teenage pregnancy, and training skilled doctors. Through his work as a physician, medical educator, and community leader, he has made immense contributions that have improved the lives of all those he has touched.

Within the field of medicine, he has been recognized by his peers as a giant in his profession, a physician of unusual stature whose judgment is trusted in dealing with the most difficult questions of medical proactive, medical ethics, and public health. His vision of health care in America is impressive, innovative, practical, and idealistic. He is an outstanding physician and an outstanding human being who has devoted his life to providing health care and opportunity to those who need help the most.

So why then did the United States Senate turn its back on Henry Foster and refuse to confirm this exemplary nominee to be Surgeon General of the United States? The nation was denied Dr. Foster's services for a simple reason: Republican opponents of a woman's right to choose filibustered it. A majority of fifty-seven senators voted to confirm Dr. Foster, but it takes sixty to break a filibuster.

Other issues were raised as a smokescreen as well—issues that were laid to rest for any fair-minded person by the extensive hearings conducted by the Senate's Labor and Human Resources Committee.

It was alleged that Dr. Foster, a black physician in the rural South in the late 1960s, knew about and acquiesced in one of the worst abuses ever committed by the United States government against black Americans. A study of syphilis, begun in 1932 by the U.S. Public Health Service at Tuskegee Institute, had instituted a deliberate policy of failing to inform black people infected with syphilis that effective treatments were available. The "scientific" rationale for this cruel, racist, and indefensible "study"—so reminiscent of Nazi Germany—was to study the progress of untreated syphilis. The allegation against Dr. Foster was preposterous. Dr. Foster convincingly refuted it and any fair judge would have thrown the charges out of court.

Other Republican opponents in the Senate chose to attack Dr. Foster's I Have a Future program. President George Bush himself thought the program was such a success that he designated it was one of his Points of Light. Dr. Foster's opponents were reduced to the unseemly position of looking for bad news with a microscope.

Those who thought the program was unsuccessful should have talked to its teenage participants. There's no doubt that they thought it worked, especially when compared to their other options in the only world they know, which is full of violence, drug abuse, schools that don't teach, joblessness, and hopelessness. The participants were proud of their accomplishments. They had graduated from high school and gone on to college. *They* thought they had a future, even if some Republican senators didn't. Henry Foster had lit a candle in their world—while his opponents preferred to curse the remaining darkness.

The syphilis study and the I Have a Future objections were makeweight arguments. At bottom, Dr. Foster was opposed by Republican senators because as an obstetrician he had performed a small number of abortions himself and was listed as the "physician of record" in others. Abortion is a constitutionally protected right. It should not have been a disqualification for the office of Surgeon General. But because Henry Foster chose to help a small number of women exercise that right, the nation was denied his service. His defeat was America's loss. No one can read this book without understanding why.

EDWARD M. KENNEDY
United States Senator
January 1997

Preface

MAKE A DIFFERENCE

This is a country that hates poverty, as indeed it should. Poverty is terrible. This is also a country that seems to hate those who are poor, punishing women and children rather than serving them.

A 1996 UNICEF study reported that about 585,000 women die as a consequence of childbirth worldwide each year and that millions of women, perhaps as many as 18 million, suffer from some serious illness or injury. In the United States, there are 4 million births every year, 1 million to women nineteen years old and younger. According to a recent study the cost to the citizenry of dealing with the social problems resulting from teenage pregnancy is an astounding $29 billion a year. There is no doubt that we have a tremendous problem to address, and wringing our hands is just not going to get us anyplace. We have to do something productive, and soon.

So much of the tragedy associated with the illness and death of women and children is preventable. We need to take care of our children. The President of the United States has spoken about teenage pregnancy as one of the primary problems confronting the nation. We in this country must make a pledge to ourselves, and to our children, that their welfare is a priority. And then we must make a difference.

One of the reasons that I was nominated for the position of Surgeon General in 1995 was that I had developed a successful program for offering deprived and poor children a sense of hope. No child deserves to be hopeless, not a single one, black or white, poor or rich. My nomination got stalled in the political machinery, which was a disappointment to me. There were programs and policies I would have liked to institute which I hoped might have improved the health status in this country, especially for our youth. But becoming a minor celebrity has turned out to have many advantages, not the least of which is that I find myself invited to speak about teenage pregnancy prevention and health-care reform all over the country.

More and more I discover that when information is offered, and problems explained, people are eager to do something to help our children, something that offers them the promise of a better future. The I Have a Future program that I developed for the at-risk inner-city youth of Nashville receives dozens of calls a month from across the nation because other people too want to offer their children a better future. I believe that the notoriety that the nomination gave me has been a blessing in disguise.

People are curious about me. They ask me not only what my ideas are on medical issues facing the nation but also how I arrived at my beliefs, what my personal experiences were that led me to my present views. As an African-American doctor, I have lived through a most interesting and exciting time—from the stormy decades before and during the civil rights movement to our present crisis in health care. My story is one of racism transcended and medical care reconceived, of moving from the poverty of the Deep South to the hallowed halls of Congress, of successful interventions and some failures, of working with people who don't have the resources to care for themselves.

I am hoping that *Make a Difference* will satisfy those who are curious. In telling about my life, especially my medical career, I'd like to portray how a mixture of pragmatism and idealism can work in concert to effect change. In rethinking the health care of the United States, the poor and underserved need to be championed, their voices heard. I want to add my voice to theirs.

Acknowledgments

I am grateful to the many people who assisted me in the preparation of this book, who offered their reminiscences, gave of their valuable time, and allowed me to impose upon their kindness. Most especially, I am eternally grateful to Alice Greenwood whose linguistic skills, intelligence, work ethic, wit, and genuine humanity facilitated this book's coming to fruition. Thank you, Alice. And without the inspiration, business acumen, and keen intellect of Leigh Haber, this book would never have become a reality. Thank you, Leigh. Also, I am appreciative to Stacey Woolf and to Flip Brophy for helping pilot this project and to Loretta McGovern for her early input.

Many others gave of their time and energy by participating in interviews. Particularly, I thank: Thelma Walker Brown, Thomas Calhoun, Terry Cole, Lorraine Greene, Ruby Hearn, Julia Lear, Emory Mazique, Leslie McKnight, Calvin Peters, Louis Rabb, David Satcher, Tracey Thornton, and Linda Williams.

My Washington experience was buffered and rendered less difficult by many sage and helpful individuals, namely: Mike Berman, Frank Billingsley, Mattye Boddie, Tim Boddie, Erskind Bowles, Carolyn Mosley Braun, Walt Broadnax, Roger Bulger, Bob Clement, President Clinton, Hillary Clinton, Ezra Davidson, Darwin Davis, Marty Davis, Vel Davis, Linda DePugh, Christopher Dodd, Jennifer Dudley, Marian Wright Edelman, Peter Edelman, Neil Eggleston, Rosalyn Epps, Charles Epps, Dianne Feinstein, Debbye Fine, Harold Ford, Harold Fox, Bill Frist, Mark Gearan, Vice President Al Gore,

Tipper Gore, Bobby Greenfield, Wilma Greenfield, Ralph Hale, Ruth Hanft, Tom Harkin, Alexis Herman, Lenora Holland, Pete Hollis, Vince Hutchins, I Have a Future youth, Jim Jeffords, Ben Johnson, Ted Kennedy, Woody Kessel, Jerry Klepler, Jack Kress, Chyrl Lander, Cres Lander, Avis Leavell, Vivian Leavell, Walter Leavell, Phil Lee, Audrey Manley, Ray Martinez, Clayton McKindra, Barbara Mikulski, Fitzhugh Mullan, Pattie Murray, Marian Osterweis, Herb Nickens, Elena Nightingale, Mary Pearse, Warren Pearse, Clayborne Pell, John Podesta, Dan Porterfield, John Ruffin, Donna Shalala, Paul Simon, Al Simpson, Clay Simpson, Wallace Charles Smith, Louis Stokes, Ginger Sullivan, Louis Sullivan, Kevin Therm, Sherman Tribble, Reed Tuckson, Harold Varmus, Donna Wachter, Ann Walker, Bill Walton, Flavia Walton, Allan Weingold, Ann Wentz, Paul Wellstone, Barbara Whitfield, Evelyn Wilbanks, George Wilbanks, Marilyn Yager, and Jim Youngblood.

Others who were most supportive and to whom I am indebted for their friendship are: Janice Barbee, Rudy Barbee, Frank Boehm, Julie Boehm, Phil Bourne, Phil Bredesen, Thomas Brooks, Phil Brown, Sadie Brown, Ernest Burnell, Betty Burnett, Lonnie Burnett, June Dobbs Butts, Hortense Calhoun, Mike Carrera, Elijah Carter, Janice Carter, Ralph Cazort, Jean Cazort, Tony Cebrun, Cecilia Chambers, Fred Chambers, Freddie Chambers, Mary Cheatham, Steve Cheatham, Dan Chester, Earl Clay, Alice Combs, Julius Combs, Collene Conway-Welch, Henry Cooper, Jim Daniell, Lois DeBerry, Roscoe Dixon, Calvin Dowe, Ken Edelin, Betty Edwards, Delmare Edwards, Joycelyn Elders, Oliver Elders, Connie Elliott, Riley Elliott, Steve Entman, Alonzo Epps, Bea Epps, Clarence Epps, Edgar Epps, James Epps, Janet Epps, Lorenzo Epps, Marilyn Epps, Gene Farley, Linda Farley, Johnny Ford, Bernice Gray, Fred Gray, Barbara Green, Charles Edward Green, Elwyn Grimes, Colette Grimes, Ben Haimowitz, Pat Haimowitz, Joe Hampton, Axel Hansen, Elnora Hansen, Linda Hare, Clarissa (P. D.) Harmon, Jim Harmon, Thelma Harper, Bailey Hill, George Hill, Joe Hill, John Hill, Kim Hill, Louis Hill, Myrna Hill, Nora Hill, Sadie Hill (deceased), Yolanda Hill, Carlton Huitt, John Hume, Henry (Sonny) Johnson, Leon Johnson,

Rosalyn Johnson, David Jones, Fred Jones, Hortense Jones, Harry Jonas, Harold Jordan, Gerri Jordan, Florence Kidd, Kermit Krantz, Bernadine Lacy, Edwina Lee, Nora Mazique, Betty McCant, Leslie McCant, Charles McGruder, Leatrice McKissick, Barbara Moore, Don Moore, Jr., Gene Moore, Juel Moore, Karen Moore, Robin Moore, Willie Mott, Philip Nicholas, Vi Nicholas, Winston Parris, Betty Patton, Ben Payton, Dan Pellegrom, Theresa Perkins, Frank Perry, Jr., Frank Perry, Sr. (deceased), Helena Perry, Stephanie Perry, Sheila Peters, Jerry Pierre, Henry Ponder, Bill Prather, Liz Prather, Bob Prince, Jimi Prince, Judd Randolph, Julius Richmond, Fred Robbins, David Rogers (deceased), Jeannie Rosoff, Ken Shine, Dan Thompson, Harold Thompson, Suzanne Thompson, William (Sonny) Walker, Carol Wall, Levi Watkins, Oba White, Verla White, Marybelle Whiteman, Sammy Whiteman, Charles Whitten, Eloise Whitten, Avon Williams, Edward (E. B.) Williams, Dodd Wilson, Deborah Wolfe, Eddie Wynn, and Mable Wynn.

Certainly there were others who played various roles in this endeavor who are not formally acknowledged at this time. For those with whom I did interact and are not listed, I ask your indulgence and remain grateful for your input.

HENRY W. FOSTER, JR., M.D.

PART I

EDUCATION
IS THE KEY

CHAPTER ONE

Learn to Write the Stories

PINE BLUFF

"I'm not afraid," I said. "Let me try."

I was seven years old and I thought I would burst with excitement. My father, a high school science teacher, had convinced a local pilot to give his students individual airplane rides—a rare experience for anyone, and remarkable for black high school kids in the 1930s. "Physics in action," he called it. We were standing close together in Tony's field, a little grass strip that ran parallel to U.S. Highway 79 in Pine Bluff, Arkansas, and I was absolutely mesmerized, watching each takeoff with that heady mixture of wonder and terror that accompanies a child's experience of the extraordinary.

The next ride of the day was coming up, the thirteenth one, and the big kids were nervous. No one was particularly eager to volunteer for what might prove to be an unlucky flight in a seemingly unreliable contraption. But I was. I knew I wanted to do it, and no superstitious silliness was stronger than that desire. It was a few minutes before anyone stepped forward, enough time for me to make myself heard. "Let me have a turn! Let me go!" Finally the next student was ready to claim his ride, and because I had been so eager—and because I was so small—I got to sit between his knees.

That first flight seemed like a miracle to me. I couldn't believe we were airborne. In fact, I felt as if we were standing still, completely stationary, and it was the earth that was rushing away from us.

This was a powerful lesson, and not solely about physics. I saw, although I couldn't articulate it then, that a change in perspective can make the world look different, that taking a chance was well worth the risk. For a little boy growing up in the deeply segregated South, my father's gift to me that day, to all of us, was the realization that anything was possible, if only we were imaginative enough and brave enough to meet the challenge.

It didn't hurt any either that the boy whose powerful legs held me tightly during that first ride was Wiley Branton, who grew up to become a prominent civil rights lawyer and dean of Howard University's law school.

Decades later, when I became a doctor and was working to improve the lives of the rural poor in Alabama and the disaffected adolescents of Nashville, I wanted to offer the same kind of gift—a change in perspective, a sense of hope, the thrill of excitement in the challenges the future held. The poor and underserved, the young people who have given up, needed to know that life held possibilities, and they needed, just as I did so long ago, someone strong to support them through the unfamiliar and frightening parts. I wanted to be that someone. My life's work has been a product of that desire.

The pleasure of flying was not the only life lesson my father taught me. Henry Wendell Foster, Sr., was fierce in his belief that education was the key to unlock the doors that were closed to blacks because of segregation, racism, and bigotry. He felt passionately, and communicated that passion to me, that education would be the Trojan horse that would cause a flawed system to crumble.

My father was a good teacher, and he was very articulate about why blacks were the object of racist discrimination. Segregation, he would explain, was a system designed by white people to subjugate others who could equal or surpass what they did. And the way they established control, and retained it, was by trying to prevent blacks from becoming educated. "If black people are as lacking in intelligence as white people say they are," my father would ask, "why was it virtually a capital offense to teach slaves how to read and write?" He said that white people didn't want black people to be successful, not because they couldn't, but precisely because they could. So it behooved us, my older sister Doris and me, if we were going to beat the odds and conquer the system, to get ourselves the best education we could.

My father spoke directly from his own experience. His mother, my Grandma Hattie, was born a mere sixteen years after slavery ended, and never had more than a fourth-grade education. Yet she devoted herself to making sure her children had choices that she never had. After her husband deserted the family, she moved to Pine Bluff, a rather plain town on the Arkansas River, and worked as a domestic. A small town of about 20,000 people, Pine Bluff had a black land-grant college, Arkansas AM&N (Agricultural, Mechanical, and Normal), now the University of Arkansas in Pine Bluff. Hattie wanted her two children to grow up in the environment of a college community, believing that their proximity to an educational institution would influence their values.

She was quite right. My aunt and my father grew up assuming that they would be college educated, and both pursued successful careers in education. My father graduated from Morehouse in 1928, one of the best colleges in the nation. Later he attended the University of Arkansas in Little Rock and earned his master's degree. He became a high school science teacher and a renowned athletic coach. My Aunt Mary went to Arkansas AM&N, and then to Grambling in Louisiana for her master's. She worked as the Superintendent of Colored Schools in Jefferson County, Arkansas.

My mother, Ivie, also believed that her children should be very well educated. Her own parents, both teachers, were themselves college graduates, which was a rare circumstance for black people in the early part of this century. Her parents expected her to do well in school and develop her talents, and she expected the same of us. My grandparents believed that my mother should have the capacity to support herself, and they told her to prepare for the possibility of having to raise children alone. "You can never predict the future," they would say. Prophetic words, as it turned out. My mother's mother died unexpectedly, shortly after the birth of her eighth child, when my mother was only twelve years old.

My mother's life held no such tragic surprises. When she was in school in Tuskegee, she met and later married my father, and they decided to settle in Pine Bluff. They lived happily together for twenty-seven years until my father died. The only complaint I ever heard from her about Pine Bluff was that she hated the unrelieved boredom of the delta landscape; it was depressing, she said. She missed the hills of her native Alabama, and she thought that Pine Bluff was just plain ugly.

Like Grandma Hattie, my parents believed that a good education would enable their children to have options and possibilities that they otherwise might never have. They wanted more than good schools for us; they wanted us to belong to an academic community that was intellectually stimulating and culturally sophisticated.

It was our good fortune that they did. One of the advantages of being associated with the college community was that I spent my precollege years in what was considered a laboratory school associated with the college. Our teachers, most of whom had advanced degrees, were specialists in every academic field related to children's education. They believed that with the proper fundamentals and encouragement—"good grounding," they called it—children should be capable of achieving virtually anything. Because our teachers were also training college students to become teachers, there were unusual amounts of academic innovation and creative teaching methods in every classroom.

Living in the midst of an enclave of black intellectuals who made up the faculty of the college—my mother taught art there—we had wonderful role models. It was easy for us to imagine that we could achieve anything we wanted, if, as my mother repeatedly reminded us, we applied ourselves to our assignments with focused concentration and energy. She wasn't as impressed with native ability as she was with good working skills. In her opinion native ability was unreliable unless coupled with good work habits; my mother didn't tolerate sloppiness or shortcuts in our schoolwork.

Although the college and the community provided us with a buffer against the worst humiliations of living in a segregated society, there was no way to completely avoid the many small degradations that were integral to daily life. We couldn't eat at the soda fountains in Woolworth's; we had to sit in the balcony of the movie theaters; we had to drink from specially labeled water fountains— all the tokens of second-class citizenry. It seemed as if we were born into a racist climate which affected every aspect of life. My mother had to give birth to her children at home because the public hospital two blocks away wouldn't accept black maternity patients. Luckily we were born without need of emergency care, thanks to the training and skill of Dr. Frank Bryant, Sr., who graduated from Meharry Medical College around the turn of the century.

Interactions with mainstream white society were fraught with small yet intolerable insults. I can remember my father's shiver of fury when we walked into a store in downtown Pine Bluff and the proprietor would ask him, "What can I do for you, *boy?*" and then turn to the white customer standing next to us and say, "Can I help you, *sir?*" Our strongest weapon against such assaults was to avoid whatever interactions we could and to live within the confines of our own community as much as possible.

In that community, the teachers, doctors, lawyers, ministers, and businesspeople had such a profound respect for their own values, and felt such a deep revulsion for the racism that scarred their lives, that they sheltered us, the children, from the worst of it. They wanted to show us, by example, that we could live as if there really were liberty and justice for all. With their help, we managed to grow up in Pine Bluff thinking that we were as good as, if not better than, anybody else.

My parents did everything possible to foster our self-esteem. Looking back now, I realize how difficult it must have been for them—intelligent, well educated, and capable—to suffer the indignities of segregation. It was less of a problem for me because I had the advantage of their protection. I grew up happily, in a lovely house on seventeen acres of land on the outskirts of town, a house filled with books, art, and music and a genuine sense of well-being.

My father kept the American Constitution on display in our living room as a constant reminder of our freedom. I can remember reading it as a child while he proclaimed: "Your freedom and justice are in this document. It's all there to set you free. But it's locked in, and the key to getting it out"—here he would tap his forehead—"is an educated mind." Two historic black newspapers, the Pittsburgh *Courier* and the Chicago *Defender,* were required reading for us because they offered real-life examples of the productivity and success of black Americans which were totally undocumented in mainstream newspapers. My parents wanted their children to know the truth about how black people were contributing their talents to this country.

The college laboratory school that I attended was as committed to celebrating African-American culture and its contribution to the history of the United States as were my parents. Ever since I can remember, in February, as part of Negro History Month, founded by Carter G. Woolson, we had to do reports about the important black figures in American history: Sojourner Truth, Frederick Douglass, Benjamin Banneker, and many others. Their achievements were never mentioned in our textbooks, but our teachers made sure we knew about them. Our class projects were designed to promote the idea that we belonged to a culture of capable people whose talents were shackled by an unfair social structure.

To motivate us, my father would tell a story about an African youth who, because he was unusually bright, got accepted into the missionary school that the smart white kids attended. Each day when the child came home from school, his father would ask him how his day had gone. When questioned one particular day, the boy looked very pensive and seemed disturbed. His father sensed something was troubling him and inquired about it. "You know, Dad," the boy said. "We go to the mission school and the missionaries tell us stories about the lions and the great white hunters. The lion is the king of the jungle, right? How come in all these stories the lions always lose? You would think that *sometimes* they would win."

The father put his arm around his son's shoulders and said, "Look, son, until the lions learn how to write the stories, they are always going to be the losers." We knew why there were no African-Americans in the history texts of this country, and we knew it wasn't because there were no important African-Americans. We just had to learn to write the stories too.

Our little school offered us a working lesson in diversity because the student population was composed of college faculty children and those from the surrounding community who were primarily from poor laboring families. It was obvious that I had many more advantages than some of these kids, and equally clear that many of them were just as smart and as capable as I was. It was impossible not to see that bright kids were sometimes poor and not so bright kids often came from the best parts of town. Those who did well in school, from both sections of the community, went on to college, and those who weren't as academically successful pursued some kind of specialized training.

Regardless of our academic standing, we all learned the pleasure and self-respect that come with doing a job well. Our teachers communicated to us that they believed that every child had value and every enterprise had dignity. Looking back now, I see what a powerful asset it was to have people truly invested in our successes, as our teachers were in all of ours. It was as if the teachers had a mission; they believed in our capacity, and so we learned to believe in our capacity too. I never wanted to disappoint them, and I am pretty sure that the other kids felt just as I did.

The economic and social heterogeneity of the school benefited us in many ways, most of which we were unconscious of at the time. For instance, it was important to our teachers that we be able to maneuver within the system, which meant we all had to be fluent in "operative" English. Each student learned how to read, write, and speak standard English in school. In my home, in fact, we were monitored very closely to ensure that our grammar was perfect, and we discovered early on that expressing ourselves the "right" way would be to our advantage.

The teachers at the college school were smart enough to know that the language of successful interaction with mainstream society was not the same thing as the language of everyone's home and family. A more vernacular English was spoken by much of the community, and was never degraded or disavowed by our teachers. They were well aware that it makes no sense to shame people about the way they speak; if people are humiliated about their speech, they simply stop speaking outside their own small group. We were taught quite deliberately to become "bilingual" so that we would be equipped to function in whatever kind of society we found ourselves, schooled or not. No doubt the teachers themselves were adept at manipulating different speaking styles, and experienced firsthand the benefits of doing so.

I was perfectly aware that not everybody was as lucky as I was, that some of my friends had fathers who were in jail, or alcoholics, or absent. Certainly many of my friends had fewer material things than I did. Nonetheless, I shared their lives and they shared mine. There was never any sense of elitism in the school or in my home. On the contrary, my parents made it clear to me that my life was full of advantages and that I had an obligation to, as they would say, "give something back." It was expected of me.

It was also expected that I be responsible, disciplined, and ambitious. My father was a strict taskmaster, believing that hard work was good for a man—and a man-in-training, as he thought of me. My mother was in charge of the emotional quality of life in our house; she was the one who offered hugs of support or quiet words of encouragement. My father felt that his responsibility was to train me to survive, and his work ethic, which was considerable, was expected to be mine too.

He was not much of an admirer of idle hands either, so while other kids were out playing ball and hanging out, at twelve years of age I became his partner in our newly established poultry business. My father was an extremely creative and enterprising man, and during World War II, he saw an opportunity to make extra money. Meat was rationed, but poultry wasn't, and he put together a big business enterprise quickly and competently. We had buildings constructed and set up galvanized brooders for the chicks and hired people to help out with the actual handling of the chickens. We sold eggs as well as poultry, calling ourselves "Foster and Son"; our slogan was: "From the nest to the table."

I was in charge of the business end of the enterprise. My father wanted me to learn to handle responsibility and I took the job seriously. Since I did the purchasing and was in charge of sales and delivery, I was forced to interact with the local businesspeople and the individuals who wanted our products. I found that it was a business asset that I was never very shy.

The poultry business of Foster and Son was not a small venture. There were many weeks when we would sell several hundred chickens, over a thousand a month, and countless eggs. On Fridays, when I got home from school, it was my job to call our customers for their orders; then on Saturdays I would drive around and make the deliveries. It didn't seem peculiar to me that at thirteen years old I was driving. It was simply necessary, and so I did it. No one in town seemed to mind that I was so young and behind the wheel; everyone knew who I was and that I was driving around on important business.

There were occasional breaks in the demanding routine, which I was pleased to take advantage of. Sometimes people wouldn't be in to receive their delivery, and I would need to return later in the day. In my enterprising way, I would go to the movies to pass the time until I had to go back again. The chickens and eggs were on ice, so I knew they could keep for a few hours. Once I went to the movies with a bag full of money, which I managed to forget in the theater. Panicked, I rushed back and found it exactly where I had left it. I don't think I would have been happy to explain lost money to my father, and I was certainly very careful after that incident.

I know my father believed that he was teaching me important life skills. He was much less demanding of my sister, whom he expected my mother to train for life. Although I often hated working so hard, most of the chores were fun, and some even interesting. Learning to drive and being encouraged to be entrepreneurial at such an early age gave me a great deal of confidence. Being forced to interact with people in such a practical way improved my social and communication skills. Just the enormity of the enterprise for a youngster was a lesson in itself, and in later years the capacity I acquired for enduring a long day of hard work served me well.

Unfortunately, no matter how successful and happy we were, there was usually an incident which reminded us that we were only peripherally tolerated by the larger culture, and we had better remember our place. I can recall our disappointment when my father and I tried to join a feed-purchasing cooperative in Fort Smith, Arkansas, and were refused entry, as if it was a private club rather than a business venture. No one bothered to fancy up our rejection either; it was simple cold racism.

I was lucky to have a best friend, Emory, to share my life in Pine Bluff, or I suspect it might have been lonely being such a young business executive. He was a year ahead of me in school; but unlike the other kids who had more freedom, he had chores and unusual responsibilities just as I did. Our fathers believed in a very stringent work ethic for their sons, and thought that the road to success was paved with hard work. I think we each felt less isolated because there was another person who shared a similar schedule: we did our chores, went to school, and came home and worked some more. Emory's family ran a restaurant at the college, the Lion's Den, and that's where he worked, opening up, cleaning up, whatever was needed. Between his store duties and my chickens, it's a wonder we had time for anything, but we found a way to forge a lifetime friendship.

On weekends, we would sleep over at each other's houses and listen to music on the radio. Each of us collected records, hundreds of 78s, which we shared and swapped. Our love of music did not extend to the music lessons our parents mandated, however, and without informing either of our families, we decided that playing football would be a better use of our time than taking our piano class. When our parents discovered what we had been doing, we both had hell to pay.

Along with music, we shared a love of airplanes. During the war years especially, when we could see many planes flying overhead, we would rush outside to identify them. Or we would play at combat. Emory was the navigator; I was always the pilot. I couldn't get enough of anything that had to do with planes. I had been flying with my father's class every year, and sometimes I could talk Tony (of Tony's airfield) into giving me an extra private ride.

I don't know what I liked better, the flying or the physical planes themselves. I was always in the midst of constructing elaborate models out of balsa wood. It took acute concentration to put these complicated planes together, and I found making them an absorbing hobby. I liked the fine handwork required to patiently fit one tiny part into another. Emory thought I was nuts to enjoy this. Making model planes seemed like work to him, but I loved it. At one time I had forty-two model planes hanging in my room. It was only in later years that I wondered if working with the intoxicating glue had something to do with my pleasure.

From time to time, Emory and I would feel the burden of our work schedules; there was too much dreary hard work, too much serious responsibility, simply too much required of young children. It almost broke Emory's spirit. He wanted to run away from home and join the service when we were about fourteen, but his mother talked him out of it, saying that we would be going on to college in just a few years and this drudgery would be in our pasts. It wouldn't have occurred to either of us that we could just say no to our fathers or tell them that we would rather be out playing. Certain things were expected of us. Period. And so we did them.

I think I was saved from feeling crushed by the demands of the work because my father was very supportive of me. I could usually get a smile out of him, and I knew that he was proud of the way I was developing. His pleasure in me did not make for good sibling relations, however, and my sister Doris never tired (or so it seemed then) of torturing me. She had been the apple of my father's eye before I was born and she adored him. I don't think she ever got over her dismay at having to share him with me. In spite, one day, when I was working on a big delicate model plane and had almost finished it, she ripped it out of my hands and sat down hard on it, destroying weeks of work. She was four years older than I was and it was pretty hard to retaliate. Eventually I got big enough or she lost interest in provoking me, and we lived under a shaky truce.

My father was not one to offer many compliments, and I sensed rather than heard directly that he loved me very much. Men like my father and Emory's didn't express their emotions overtly. In an odd way, his demands on me and his expectations that I meet them encouraged me to excel. I wanted his approval, and tried to get it by working even harder than he expected. So I attacked my chores with great enthusiasm and I was very diligent about succeeding in my schoolwork.

When World War II broke out, my father stopped teaching high school science and went to work for the war effort, building incendiary bombs at the Pine Bluff Arsenal. He was made head of a unit because he had a degree in chemistry from Morehouse College. Was I ever proud when a picture of him appeared in the Pittsburgh *Courier,* standing next to a huge bomb, with the caption: "Here's a present for you, Adolf." It was only years later that I came to realize that my father wasn't solely responsible for building most of the bombs that destroyed Europe.

It was during the war that I learned about the Tuskegee Airmen. A former student of my father's, Herbert Clark, had been chosen to be part of that elite group of black fighter pilots. In fact, several of the young men my father had motivated through high school—and who had had their first taste of flying as part of his science class— became part of the new unit. The story of the Airmen captured my imagination and never lost its hold on me. I so admired what I heard about their courage, grit, spirit, and determination. For a child, this was the real stuff of adventure stories. The Airmen covered themselves with glory during the war, never losing a single bomber to enemy aircraft when they served as support, and our community was proud as could be to know several of the members of the corps.

The war became very vivid for me when Herbert got shot down while on a mission in northern Italy. Suddenly I actually knew someone who flew a plane and was in enemy hands, maybe even dead. No one was clear about what had happened to him; he was seen parachuting from his burning plane and became one of the many on the list of "Missing in Action."

Herbert's father, Jeremiah Clark, was the pastor of our church, the St. Paul Baptist Church, and our families were friends and colleagues—Mrs. Clark taught mathematics at the college—as well as neighbors. Every Sunday in church she would pray for her son's safety, absolutely sure that her baby was still alive. As if in answer to her prayers, Herbert was found alive when the Allies went into Italy and he was able to rejoin his family for Christmas in 1944. I was enthralled by his war stories, and listening to Herbert tell them, when he had dinner at our house, helped me to decide that when I grew up, I would be a pilot.

Between my father's work at the arsenal and Herbert's exploits, I was sure the war was being fought entirely by black men. I couldn't believe it when I discovered that these same pilots, who had been so lauded for their extraordinary success and bravery during the war, came home to an America that refused to let them work at what they did so well. At that time, there was not a single airline in the United States that would hire a black pilot. It was a bitter pill that I am not sure I have ever quite swallowed. As a practical matter, this discovery made me realize I had to give up my dream of becoming a professional pilot.

As much as I had hoped to study aeronautical engineering and become a pilot, it would have been futile to train myself to be unemployed. I was my father's son, and very practical. I knew I wanted to make a contribution, and I also wanted to get some remuneration for my efforts. So I had to rethink my options. I looked around me and saw African-Americans who were physicians, dentists, teachers, morticians, and businesspeople. Becoming a doctor seemed a way to do some good and make a living. My parents had taught me that I had an obligation to try to leave this world in better shape than I'd found it, and a career in medicine seemed an excellent way to do that.

One of my father's best friends, Clyde Lawlah, was also our doctor. He had graduated from Morehouse College a few years earlier than my father and went on to the University of Chicago for his medical degree, one of the few black people to do so. Although I am sure he could have gone anywhere in the country to open a practice, he came back to Pine Bluff. All the time I was growing up, whenever I could, I would accompanied him when he made his house calls. Mine was the weighty responsibility of carrying his medical bag; it seemed very important to me, this being a doctor, and I liked it.

Also, I was very impressed with what medical treatment could accomplish. My dog Blackie, who was a wonderful friend to me and whom I loved unashamedly, got lost once in the woods. We found him caught in an animal trap with his leg badly hurt, and Aunt Mary and I rushed him to the vet. The only way the vet could save Blackie's life was to amputate his leg, and I was devastated, because I thought the dog would never be the same, that he would somehow be ruined. But he wasn't. In no time at all, he was back to his old self, chasing rabbits and welcoming me home from school. After a while, I forgot that he was maimed; he was perfect just the way he was. That incident must have taught me something about medical possibilities; I certainly never looked at disabilities in the same way again.

What really cemented my decision to become a doctor was observing at close range a medical emergency with a happy ending. My mother's oldest sister, Odell, developed a very serious condition in pregnancy, called eclampsia, which caused her to convulse. A convulsion is terrible to see, even if you are a doctor, and to a young high school kid, it was totally frightening. And I knew that there was a real chance that she could die. Terrified, I accompanied my mother to the university hospital, where the doctors worked hard to save her and her twin sons, Alonzo and Lorenzo, my first cousins. I thought to myself that this was a good thing to be able to do.

The war years brought changes into my household. My mother had been offered a government job with the Rural Housing Authority, some distance away, making a salary four times what she was earning at the college. The technique she used when applying for the job tickled me because I had never consciously realized just how savvy she was. The job was to teach poor rural women homemaking skills, especially about food preparation, and knowing how to "can" was a prerequisite for the job. Crucial to proper canning is that there be no bacteria in the can, and my mother, who was very observant, noticed that a can which had not been prepared properly would swell within a day or two. So she prepared her cans for the federal authorities who were evaluating the applicants for this position, but she waited a day before sending them off. She was hired because all her cans were perfect, not one of them was spoiled. I thought my mother remarkably clever.

My mother took this new job very seriously. If she did her work well, then poor rural women would have food supplies that would take them through the winter, food that they might otherwise not have. There was no refrigeration in the homes of these poor people and thus canning and dehydrating techniques were very valuable to them. A few homes had indoor bathtubs, which were somewhat rare in that area, and my mother had to chide the owners of these houses not to use the tubs to store food.

I went with her on occasion, especially during the summer, and I was struck with how terribly deprived these women were, and I was impressed by how little they had, how meager were their lives, and by how desperately my mother wanted to help them. She was always most respectful when she spoke to the women, very sensitive to their feelings, and very compassionate when she spoke to me about them. To her mind, and to mine, these poor people were in need, and because we had so much more than they did, it was our duty to try to help them as much as we could. I knew she really cared about their lives and about the cruelty of their poverty.

I had never been exposed to that level of deprivation, and I'm sure, accompanying my mother into these areas, and seeing the tremendous gap between their lives and my own, gave me, at an impressionable age, unusual insight into the inequities of services in this country. I saw with my own eyes that many people, through no fault of their own, live in an indescribably rudimentary way, struggling just to have their basic needs met. It made me somewhat uncomfortable to then return to my middle-class life; it felt as if I were turning my back on people who needed help, but I also remember how proud I was of my mother's capacity to make their lives better.

In order to do this job, my mother had to live away from home all week, but she came back on weekends. Since my father was so busy at the arsenal and we were both spending time tending to the poultry business, it was decided to send my sister to a posh boarding school in North Carolina, the Palmer Memorial Institute. This was fine with me.

I enjoyed this chance to be alone with my father, who was, to my mind, the best and bravest person I knew—in every way my personal hero. When I was about twelve, Emory and I rode our bikes across the Arkansas River, and because it was hot, we stopped at a local store to get a soda. The proprietor, a white man, took a look at us and began waving a gun around, which he said was loaded. He pointed it at us and threatened us with it, in a kind of mocking way. We cleared out of there pretty fast.

When I reported this incident to my father later in the day, I hardly recognized him for the rage that took over this usually controlled and civilized person. He went straight to our lawyer, Harold Flowers, and we all got into our car and rode over to the store in a hurry. My father wanted that man arrested on the spot for pulling a gun on me, and it was only after the proprietor offered me and my father many apologies and promised never to scare innocent children again that my father was willing to let it be.

I grew up with the wonderful knowledge that there was nothing my father wouldn't do for me—including face off a white guy with a gun. It's not every child who has a chance to see that his father would die to keep someone from harming him. He made me feel completely safe from danger.

Indeed I always felt perfectly at ease in my community while I was growing up, even though I lived in the deeply segregated South of the 1940s and 1950s. We couldn't sit at the store counters in town, but this didn't seem such a hardship, because we had our own restaurants, which we liked just fine. When we were forced to sit in the balcony at the movie theaters, we discovered certain advantages to that position. Emory and I would find our seats upstairs on Saturday afternoons and cheerfully take turns throwing popcorn and other things down on the heads of the white kids. It didn't seem too bad.

We had our own black-owned movie theater in town where we could see wonderful films—and where we could sit wherever we pleased. The Vester Theater was owned by a local mortician, a multi-millionaire named P. K. Miller, who named the theater for his wife. Mr. Miller made his fortune because he knew very well that black people, including poor black people, have a healthy respect for death, and that meant spending money on funerals. He expanded a small business into a chain of mortuaries, and because he loved the movies, he wanted a theater where he could watch—and sit—wherever he liked. As children, we were in awe of his accomplishments, and this theater was important to us because we saw that it was possible to fulfill dreams and even to get rich in the process.

The black community in Pine Bluff seemed like a self-contained universe, with its own schools, restaurants, movie houses, businesses, funeral parlors, and churches. But when we ventured out of the community and interacted with the majority culture, we came face-to-face with discrimination, so we left our community only when absolutely necessary. I hated it when, as a young boy, I had to stand up in a bus which was full of empty seats. If the "colored" section was all taken, and the "white only" seats were empty, I still had to stand up in front of an empty seat. That seemed awfully stupid to me.

Consequently, I stopped riding the buses, as did most of my friends. We had bikes which could take us to the places we needed to go. And feet. In fact, the black community really boycotted the buses in an informal way. No one talked about it, and it certainly wasn't organized, but most people avoided riding on the city buses altogether. I can't remember either of my parents, or any of their friends for that matter, ever taking a bus. But then we always had a car to get around in, so avoiding the bus was no great sacrifice to us, as it might have been to others.

Emory and I would walk the few miles to the movies and enjoy the freedom to visit. These walks also allowed me the pleasure of scaring him out of his wits. He was phobic about snakes, absolutely terrified, so I would throw a stick into the bushes as we walked along, then jump back and yell, "Snake, snake!" and watch him take off screaming. Of course, he waited for an opportunity to even the score, but I didn't give him one. I can't remember if I really wasn't afraid of anything, but I certainly let Emory think that was the case.

He graduated the year before I did as valedictorian of his class and went on to Howard University. Although I missed him, I was very busy myself applying to college and preparing for my own graduation. I was pleased to be the valedictorian of my class, following in Emory's footsteps, and I know my family was proud too. The speaker at my graduation was Dr. Charles Hicks, Superintendent of Public Colored Schools for the state, and I remember his message that we should go forth into the world and become whatever we wanted to be, that nothing should be able to stop us.

I was on my way to Morehouse College, my father's alma mater, and was eager to take up Dr. Hicks's challenge.

CHAPTER TWO

Dare to Dream

MOREHOUSE COLLEGE

The summer before I started at Morehouse, my sister Doris did me a surprisingly good turn. Having just graduated from Talladega College in Alabama, perhaps she felt charitable toward her little brother, who was starting out. I was working at George Hestand's grocery store in the unglamorous position of stockboy, pretty much biding my time until I could leave for Atlanta. My father had decided to wind down the poultry business because I wouldn't be able to manage it long distance and he couldn't handle it alone.

Doris suggested that instead of wasting the summer doing nothing to improve my mind, I should read. Read anything, she said, just read. She told me that the first thing that would happen to me when I got to college was that I would be given various placement exams, the results of which would determine how much latitude I would have in choosing my courses. All these tests were really based on reading skills, she said, and the only way to improve these skills was to read. Easy for her to say; she loved reading. I took her advice to heart and spent the summer reading Mickey Spillane's Mike Hammer mysteries, Erskine Caldwell novels, and whatever else I could find lying around.

As it turned out, this was exactly the right thing to do, because I managed to score above the thirteenth-grade level in reading, which allowed me to be unrestricted in how many credits I could take and in my choice of courses. As a premed student, I had such a demanding schedule that anything I could do to relieve the pressure was most welcome, but I also wanted to fulfill my requirements as expeditiously as possible. We had a two-year foreign language requirement, and there were many humanities subjects that had to be successfully negotiated, all in addition to the science requisites. Only about one quarter of the students who started premed were able to successfully complete the rigorous curriculum.

Academics was not my top priority at Morehouse, however. As soon as I got there, I realized that I had better focus on my social situation. I was not yet seventeen years old and I looked like twelve; I was quite short, slightly chubby, and I had a bad case of adolescent acne. I didn't look—or feel—much like a college man. To make matters even worse, the members of the class included many World War II veterans; in contrast with them, I looked like an absolute baby, which was obviously not the look I was after.

It was apparent who the popular guys were, and I decided that I wanted to be one of them. Their look was very macho, very hip, and I knew that their swaggering self-confident style and their zippy clothes weren't going to fit on my round five-foot-two frame very easily. Even though I couldn't be exactly like them, I could certainly be friends with them, and I found myself gravitating toward the members of the school's in-crowd.

I had considered myself quite the young buck back in Pine Bluff, and therefore I had a certain measure of confidence to start out with. Now I made use of what social skills I had to ingratiate myself with my new peers. I entertained them with stories and jokes, especially welcome after a long study session, when everyone was exhausted, or during our never-ending game of pinochle.

One guy in particular, Don Moore, was thought to be particularly cool because he had access to a car, and a car meant a lot of freedom in those days. Don's sister was a French professor on campus and she let him use her car whenever he wanted. His home was in La Grange, Georgia, about an hour or so from Atlanta, and it was a measure of high status to be invited to join the group which gathered at his house for weekends. Don and I were antithetical personality types; nonetheless we found we liked each other a lot, and we became the best of friends. I began joining his group for the weekend outings, and felt I had found my niche.

Being part of the hip crowd had certain disadvantages, however, because the school administration was suspicious of this group. One weekend, Don and I had been out gallivanting somewhere and returned to the college quite late, one or two o'clock in the morning. The next day we were called into the dean's office because the vending machines had been broken into and their contents stolen. Don and I had been seen walking around late. What had we to say about this? We had nothing at all to say about it.

The dean wrote a letter to our parents, informing them of the "incident." I was outraged that anyone would think that I would be dishonest. The way I was raised in Pine Bluff, if someone dropped a dollar, you were expected to run after them and return it; doing less would have been considered stealing and I was certainly no thief. My parents asked me what "this business" was about, and I told them the truth, that I had absolutely no idea. Since they were pretty confident that it was not in my nature to do anything that foolish, they let the matter drop.

Some of the other cool guys thought it their duty to teach us "innocents" about the good life. Benny Lee from Gary, Indiana, was a big man who, because he was prematurely bald, looked like he was thirty years old. I imagine that we must have been a peculiar pair walking together, he so mature looking, I so young. One night after a basketball game, we stopped at a local hangout, and unbeknownst to me, Benny had the manager of the place turn the temperature up higher and higher. I got hotter and hotter, and Benny recommended beer—and then more beer. That evening was my introduction to drinking in college and probably my one and only bout with being under the influence. It didn't appeal to me at all, either the beer or the being played with, and it didn't happen again.

Smoking was another marker of being a big college man which never appealed to me; I always hated it and thought the habit disgusting and stupid. My roommate, Bobby Anderson, of Augusta, Georgia, smoked all the time; in those days, the cigarette companies would supply people with "starter" packs and Bobby was never without a Lucky Strike. We were studying for a chemistry exam late one night when he jumped up and started rummaging through trash baskets. I couldn't imagine what he was looking for, and when I asked him, he said, "A butt."

"From the garbage?" I asked in disbelief.

A few minutes later, he was dressed in a raincoat and hat—it was pouring out. He needed to go out to get himself "some smokes." I asked him why he didn't wait till morning, and he looked at me like I was crazy. But it was pretty clear to me who was the crazy one.

I teased him constantly about his addiction. When he would finish a cigarette, I would immediately offer him a new one. Naturally, he would refuse, saying he didn't want one right then, because he had just had one. I told him that I had discovered a secret about smoking: people smoked so that they would not want to smoke. Pretty dumb, I said. I never felt like I wanted to smoke, I told him, and so he and I ended up in the same place, except that I didn't have to rummage around in trash cans or go out in a storm to get that feeling.

No matter how much I learned those first few weeks of school, there were frequent reminders that I really was a small-town boy living in a big city for the first time. I remember what a dope I was when I went to Paschel's restaurant shortly after I arrived at Morehouse and importantly ordered a steak. When the waiter brought it, I was quite upset. "What's this?" I asked, full of irritation. Whatever it was that was sitting in the middle of my plate looked like nothing that I had ever seen before.

"Steak," he answered, "as you ordered, sir."

It was a broiled T-bone steak, completely unfamiliar to me. In my house, where my mother made pan-fried steak with gravy, steak looked very different. I felt a little foolish at how prepared I had been to chew out the waiter; then decided more philosophically that a liberal education included such important points of information.

As exciting as it was to be discovering new things about the world, there were times when I missed home and the life that was so easy and familiar. Every once in a while that first year I would see a B-52 flying at a great altitude, headed west, and I would think that in a few minutes that same plane would be over Arkansas.

I was looking forward to returning to school for my sophomore year partly because I had reached a new height of five foot eight, six inches taller than the previous year, and I had also slimmed down quite a bit. Not only did I feel better about the way I looked, but I was secure in the friendships I had made. The most pleasure came from being invited to pledge a fraternity, Kappa Alpha Psi, the very chapter that had been my father's thirty years before.

Fraternity life became the center of my social activities in college. Something was always going on: dances and mixers and what were called "smokers." There were weeks of frantic activity preceding our highly celebrated Homecoming weekend. Every year we tried to produce a float for the Homecoming parade that was bigger and better than those of the other fraternities. Our Kappa Sweetheart was chosen from among the women of Spelman College, our sister school, which was located right across the street. Since Spelman had twice the number of students as Morehouse, and we were always interacting, I never experienced the isolation typical of an all-male school. I enjoyed the fraternal community greatly; it well suited my gregarious nature, so in my senior year, when I was elected polemarch, or president, of the fraternity, I embraced the responsibility with enthusiasm.

Being preoccupied with extracurricular activities and a social life meant that I was not going to be number one or even number two in my college class. Half the students who attended Morehouse were valedictorians or salutatorians of their high school class; my academic background did not make me particularly outstanding. I had determined early on that grades were not going to be my top priority, and looking back, I think I made the right choice. I was bright enough and had enough "good grounding" from Pine Bluff to do very well. These years were ones I was devoting to making the transition from boyhood to manhood. I was not ever academically irresponsible, because I wanted to get into medical school and knew the competition would be great. Also I needed to maintain a high enough grade point average to keep my student deferment from the armed forces.

One Christmas vacation, I had a terrible scare. I came home to a letter from my draft board, which said, "Greetings," please report on such and such a day to be inducted into the armed forces. I remember that my mother was fixing me my favorite meal, steak (made the old-fashioned way) with onions and rice, and as soon as I saw that letter I lost my appetite. I had never lost my appetite before.

Aunt Mary heard about this when she called to welcome me home and in no time at all had dressed herself and appeared at our house to "sort this matter out." As soon as she arrived, she told me to get in the car and off we drove to see Mr. Wade Black, who owned a florist shop and was the chairman of the local draft board. He must have been quite startled to see a short angry black woman with a young man in tow banging on the door of his most exclusive house at eleven-thirty at night.

He sleepily managed to open the door, and Aunt Mary lit right into him. She shook the letter under his nose, and said, "What's this?" Didn't he realize that her nephew was working hard to make something of himself? Did he not see all the no-account boys who were lazying around the pool hall all day with nothing to do? Why was he trying to put her nephew into the Army when he was preparing himself for medical school?

Mr. Black tried to calm her down and told her it was probably a mistake. Her anger was not so easily quelled, and she reminded him that even mistakes could be dangerous. If you get mistakenly hit by a car, you still get killed or hurt badly, she pointed out. I thought my aunt most formidable; she was every inch my father's sister. Eventually she took a breath and he told me to come to the draft board office the next morning in order to get to the bottom of this unfortunate matter. The following day we discovered that

Morehouse had inadvertently forgotten to send in my most recent transcript and thus the draft board had no record of my schooling. Morehouse was contacted, they responded right away, and the matter was resolved. My plans remained to enter the Air Force when I finished medical school, not in my junior year of college.

The core of Morehouse, for me and probably for every student, was not the wonderful camaraderie or the fun or the superior education we received. It was its extraordinary president, Benjamin Elijah Mays, who was a brilliant educator, a mover of men, an inspiring orator, and a remarkable thinker. He spoke to us once a week, and for four years I heard him with undiminished pleasure. Attendance was taken in our compulsory chapel meetings every other day of the week, but there was never any need for roll call on Tuesdays when Dr. Mays gave his talk. No one wanted to miss it.

Dr. Mays symbolized the pride of Morehouse College and even his life story was inspiring. He was born the son of slaves; yet he went to Bates College in Maine, the first African-American to ever attend. When he graduated Phi Beta Kappa, he continued his education at the University of Chicago, where he earned a doctorate in theology. This was a man who had broken barriers in his lifetime, and who believed that one could—and should—make a difference.

He lectured us about self-respect, about dignity and fairness. We were Morehouse men, from a long tradition of African-American scholars. Dr. Mays exhorted us to examine our value system; he wanted us to be sure that our actions reflected our most sincere beliefs. Why, he would ask, would any one of us ever go into a segregated movie theater? That was absurd; we didn't need to go, it wasn't food or anything else necessary to life. Since we all knew that segregation was despicable, unpardonable, didn't we realize that even such trivial acts made us passive participants in the process? I would bet no Morehouse man ever looked at a movie theater in the same way again. I certainly didn't.

With his compelling gift of oratory, there was never a sound in the chapel when he spoke, not a cough or a scraped chair. He delivered the same message over and over again: never sell yourselves short; never compromise your dreams. "The real tragedy in life is not failure," he would tell us. "Failure is part of being human. To die with dreams unfulfilled is no disgrace. But to die without dreams is intolerable." Aim high. Try hard. And then live with the consequences. It was the responsibility of Morehouse graduates to change the world; if we didn't, who would?

Every year, toward the end of the term, Dr. Mays would give a special talk to the students; we knew what was coming, and we enjoyed ourselves immensely. In chapel, students were grouped according to year: freshmen were on the upper balcony on the left, sophomores on the right. Below, the juniors were on the left and seniors on the right. Dr. Mays's recurring theme was that we take ourselves and our studies seriously, and his final lecture was a ritualized good-bye.

First he would address his remarks to the freshmen. He would tell them, "I know there are many of you who have wasted your time gallivanting in the streets when you should have been studying. But chances are, if you are really committed, you can make up for this deficit." Then in his deepest and most serious voice, he would intone, "It is your job to maximize your educational opportunities, to take advantage of this institution."

After a moment's pause, he would shift his position slightly, and turn to the sophomores. "Your college education is halfway done," he would begin. "Some of you have squandered all kinds of opportunities and your futures are beginning to look dismal. I don't know what you're going to do as a group."

He would turn toward the juniors next. "You were gallivanting in the streets when the students at Georgia Tech were preparing for the world to come. So many of you were wasting your time that it will surely be a miracle if you ever achieve anything."

We could orchestrate this speech by the time we were seniors, and we happily anticipated the next part. For us, as seniors, it was the culmination of four wonderful years of speeches. Dr. Mays would put his left hand on his left hip and very slowly raise his right hand with his index finger extended. Then he would deliberately wag that finger back and forth and back and forth for a long five seconds. He would say, with an almost palpable laugh in his voice, and with tremendous affection, "Seniors, it's too late! It's just too late for you!" We would bring down the house with cheers and applause—passing the torch to the underclassmen.

Our commencement speaker at graduation was Dr. Nathan Pusey, then president of Harvard. In his address, he told us that he had analyzed data about students and faculty from colleges all over the country. The result, he was delighted to share with us, was that more than any other institution in America, Morehouse resembled Amherst College.

After the ceremony, I went to Dr. Pusey and thanked him for his fine commencement address, and asked him, when he next spoke to the students at Amherst, to congratulate them for looking like Morehouse. I'm sure he realized that comparing us with a bastion of elite upper-class white malehood was not particularly impressive to this assemblage of Morehouse men.

My summer vacations during college permitted me the luxury of putting away my textbooks in order to explore new things. I spent a couple of summers working in Asbury Park, New Jersey, as a busboy in the Kingsley Arms Hotel, where I was able to earn enough money to take care of my school expenses for the following year. Besides its being economically wise, I did this, as so many of us did, because it was wonderful fun. College kids from the South would travel up and down the East Coast by the hundreds, taking work wherever they could get it. The beach was the best place to be, and I loved the boardwalk and the clambakes and the pretty girls.

The summer of my junior year I was determined to go to California, just for the adventure of seeing something new. My mother's brother, my Uncle Louis, was a major in the Air Force at March Air Force Base outside Riverside, California, and he had gotten me a job in the base exchange. It paid very well and I would be around planes, which I still loved. The principal of my high school, Mrs. Ruby Fischer, was traveling to California also, and when she heard of my plans, she asked me if I would be willing to help her drive her brand-new Pontiac across the country. I would be delighted to drive her brand-new car, I told her, and she knew I was a very good driver, having seen me at it since I was thirteen years old.

My job at the Air Force base was working at the soda fountain, but it quickly expanded and I became responsible for one of the big vans that drove coffee around to the pilots on duty. The country was in the midst of the Cold War in 1953, and this was a Strategic Air Command (SAC) base. There were frequent "alerts" so that the pilots, flying B-47s armed with nuclear weapons, would be in the aircraft prepared to take off at a second's notice and destroy half the world. It was no small thing to gain entry to an aircraft loaded with nuclear bombs; just to bring in coffee, I had to get a top-secret clearance.

My mother called one day to ask what was going on out there in California, because government men were going around Pine Bluff asking people all kinds of bizarre questions about me. When I told her that I was delivering coffee to men who were sitting on top of nuclear bombs, she was duly impressed. Every evening I had to go through an elaborate ritual, getting a secret password so that the armed sentries would let me on the flight line. My mother wanted to know if I was nervous about being on these airplanes, even as a delivery boy. I told her shucks, no, the only thing I was upset about was that I wasn't flying the airplanes myself.

The following year, in the summer of 1954, I did finally fly, not a B-47, but a J-3 Piper Cub. I had been taking flying lessons with an instructor at the SAC aero club, which was open to civilian employees. I knew more about flying than most novices because I understood the aerodynamics so well. All that model building and flights with Tony were providing me with dividends. After passing the written exams easily, I needed to log in enough hours with my instructor until he thought I was ready to fly solo.

My instructor was a big heavy man named Sorensen. One Sunday morning, August 29, 1954, we had been practicing touch-

and-gos. These are maneuvers in which you bring the plane to the ground, taxi for a bit, and go right back up again without ever stopping the plane. On one of these moves, Sorensen asked me to stop the plane because he wanted to go to the rest room. As he stepped off, he said, "Take it around," and I, not understanding what he meant, said, "Okay, I'll be right here waiting for you to come back."

"No," he said. "You take it around by yourself."

"Where are you going to be?" I was confused because I had only logged about seven hours' total flying time, not very much experience.

"In the rest room," he said, and smiled.

I didn't wait around for him to change his mind. Flying solo is a necessary prerequisite for getting a Department of Commerce student certificate, something like a behind-the-wheel driver's test. It is the moment of reckoning; you're all alone in the plane, no instructor by your side handling the dual controls.

I taxied the plane and took off. I got a little nervous when I realized the nose was heavy because the center of gravity changed so much when Sorensen got off, and I had to make a quick correction. Other than that the flight went remarkably smoothly, and it was just as I had imagined it would be for so many years. Right then, I determined that one day I would have my own plane and fly it all over the place. I didn't ever want to come back down to earth.

When I did touch down, Sorensen and some other guys were waiting on the tarmac to congratulate me. A tradition had developed around a student's solo flight in which the bottom of the shirt he was wearing was cut off and then labeled with his name and the date and hung up in the hangar. That little strip of cloth, along with my recently earned college diploma, made me feel as if I had really come of age. I knew I needed all the confidence I could get if I was going to manage to successfully accomplish the next challenge, medical school.

CHAPTER THREE

No Growth Without Conflict

UNIVERSITY OF ARKANSAS MEDICAL SCHOOL

In the 1950s, black students who wanted to become doctors did not have many options about where to attend medical school. Basically there were two choices, Meharry, in Nashville, Tennessee, and Howard, in Washington, D.C. These institutions had been training black doctors for nearly a century and the competition for every place within them was fierce.

The nation's other medical schools rarely accepted black students. Occasionally a black student would gain entrance, like my father's friend, Dr. Lawlah, who went to the University of Chicago, but these acceptances were few and far between, and really showed no commitment to diversity. On the contrary, such isolated acceptances served to maintain segregation in these schools by suggesting that when a really outstanding candidate applied, that person was accepted. Utter nonsense, of course; there was no shortage of outstanding candidates.

There were some mainstream medical schools that admitted black students into their programs, but only for the first two years. After that, if the students wanted to complete their training, and do their clinical practicums, they were forced to transfer to either Howard or Meharry. The rationale behind this two-year policy was that it was acceptable to have black students in a classroom with white students, but the schools wouldn't sanction black doctors actually touching and interacting with white patients. Presumably the white patients would have been made uncomfortable. In the 1950s, this kind of blatant racism was tolerated, accepted as simply the way things were.

I was not at all keen to participate in such a system, and so applied only to those schools where I would be able to complete my training. This meant that I applied to Howard and Meharry; but I also took a chance and applied to the University of Arkansas Medical School in Little Rock. I liked Arkansas and I knew what a superlative medical school it was. Winthrop Rockefeller had adopted it, and because it was so well funded in salaries, laboratories, and equipment, the school was able to attract a world-class faculty.

Of even more importance, the medical school was attempting integration, and doing so without compulsion from the law. In 1948 the first black student was admitted, Edith Irby Jones, and from that point on, there were always a few black students, and I knew one of them, Ernest Burnell, from Morehouse. At the time I was applying, there was a total of about six African-American medical students there, which was certainly better than none.

I applied and was accepted.

I had had an interview during Christmas vacation of my senior year, and even though I'd thought it had gone very well, I was still surprised when I returned to Morehouse a few days later to find a letter of acceptance waiting for me. As relieved and as happy as I was to be accepted anywhere—there were at least five applicants for each place—I thought I should wait for Howard's and Meharry's decisions before I made a final commitment. I thought that I could handle myself academically at the University of Arkansas, but I had never lived in an almost exclusively white environment and I wasn't completely sure how I would adjust to it. I feared the isolation would be stifling.

Around the time that I was struggling with this decision, I met Mrs. Daisy Bates at a reception. Mrs. Bates was one of the most influential people in the state of Arkansas, and a household name. She was president of the NAACP in Arkansas and the editor of a progressive newspaper, the *Arkansas State Press,* to which I still sub-scribe today. Her mission in life was to improve the opportunities and lives of black people in this country, beginning with education reform. She knew everything that affected issues of integration and segregation in the state of Arkansas, which included, it seemed, my early acceptance by the medical school.

Daisy Bates would hound the deans of the school, demanding to know which of the fine black students who were graduating from college that year would be accepted. She knew even before I did that year that I was one of them. After we were introduced, she said, "I understand that you are going to the University of Arkansas Med-ical School." Surprised that she should know anything about me, or my plans, I told her indeed I had been accepted but I was still unsure about whether I wanted to go there.

Mrs. Bates would have none of that. The decision was really quite clear, she told me. I had to go to Arkansas, didn't I realize that? Patiently she explained what should have been obvious, although I must admit I hadn't thought of it. If I went to Arkansas, there would be one more space for another student at one of the black universities. By attending Arkansas, I would in effect permit another black student to have the opportunity of becoming a doc-tor. When she put it that way, it seemed as if there really was no other choice to make.

I was nervous about my decision. Even though I knew I had been very well trained at Morehouse, I was still nervous. This was med-ical school, and everyone who ever talked about it joked that medical school was as close as a person can get to death without dying. Hardly reassuring. Further, there was the uncomfortable reality of being the "other," a minority for the first time in my life. Every place I had lived, or worked, or gone to school, a significant part of the population had been black. At the University of Arkansas Medical School I would have to operate in a primarily white society where I would have to eat in a separate cafeteria and drink from a separate water fountain. I was usually eager to accept challenges, but this one was daunting.

I reminded myself of my father's teachings: the system was faulty; I wasn't. The only way to prove "them" wrong was to show them just how wrong they were.

These noble sentiments deflated a bit as I looked around the medical school entering class on the first day of school and saw that literally all of the ninety-five surrounding faces were white and male. After the welcoming speeches, I made my way over to the dean, F. Douglas Lawrason, and asked him how many Negroes would be in the class (we were "Negroes" then). He put his hand on my shoulder and said, "Foster, you are it." In addition to being the only black student in the class, I realized I was also the youngest. I knew I had my work more than cut out for me.

It was lonely work too, but I was so busy and so driven to succeed that I hardly noticed the time passing. I had come to get educated, and educated I would get. My social isolation forced my commitment to my academics to be uncompromising. The workload was almost unbearable; still I drove myself to outshine everyone else. It was as if I imagined that Daisy Bates was counting on me to show the school what bright black students could accomplish, if given the chance. Between Daisy Bates, my father, and myself, the pressure on me was sometimes unbearably high.

When I felt overwhelmed I often rallied by remembering the great hardships that my cousin Clarence Davenport used to tell me about when I was a child. Clarence was one of the few blacks who had been accepted at West Point in 1939, and the rigors of his first year, the silent treatment he received from his classmates, the extraordinary physical as well as academic hurdles he had to overcome, and in almost total isolation from his peers, somehow made me feel that my situation really wasn't so terrible.

But the other students around me had each other; they had fraternities which had repositories of old exams, the "rocks" as they were called, and other assets that I didn't have access to and which might have been very useful. I wasn't invited into these fraternities and had to make do with what I did have—my textbooks and a highly developed work ethic, which I intended to use to show my classmates that their ideas about race were entirely wrong. When some of them flunked out, even those who had graduated from fancy Ivy League colleges, while I continued to do very well, I think there were a few people who might have been forced to rethink their preconceived ideas. At least I certainly hoped so.

I was not especially angry at the racist stupidities of my classmates, only somewhat frustrated. I told myself that if I had been brought up the way they had been, I might think exactly as they did. They were ignorant, that's all; they had had no exposure to anyone who was different from them. It wasn't that they were evil people, just uneducated, and I attempted to position myself as a good teacher.

I remember one of my classmates giving me a lecture on what he was pleased to call "racial pride." We were on a cadaver break, having a soda, and he was telling me about how much he admired Ralph Bunche and Jackie Robinson and other kinds of foolishness. Then he got to the punch line. He said that he was mighty proud of his race, being white, and because he was so proud, he was going to marry someone who was white; he wanted his kids to be white too. He was that proud of his race. Didn't I feel the same pride about my race?

I looked at him, and said, "Bill, I'm luckier than you, you know, because I can marry anybody I want, of any race, and my kids'll still be black. Remember genetics class? Black is dominant. Now, don't get mad at me. You made up those rules." He gave me the oddest look.

It wasn't only the students who had peculiar ideas about race. My pathology chairman, Dr. Anderson Nettleship, called me into his office one day and asked me to have a seat. He was at his desk going through a folder, and he looked up very seriously and said, "Foster, you know, I don't think Negroes are ready to study medicine."

I looked back at him just as seriously and said, "You may be right, Dr. Nettleship, but I'm sure that *I'm* ready to study medicine."

I don't know why he said that; he seemed otherwise an intelligent and fair man. Maybe he was trying to provoke me so that I would work even harder, or maybe he hoped to undermine my confidence and force me to quit school. Whatever his reason, I wanted to convince him that I was as capable as anyone, and I became even more determined to succeed. Dr. Nettleship was forced to give me one of the very rare A's in his course, and I actually think both of us were pleased by the way things worked out.

That first year I studied as I had never studied before, with intense concentration and focus. There was no time for a social life, or for any life outside my studies. I wanted to pass the examinations with the highest grades, and then to be the best doctor in the school, to show everyone, perhaps including me, that I could do it.

My commitment to my medical education made my former teachers in Pine Bluff very proud. When I came home during my first year, full of book learning, I went to visit one of my favorite teachers, Miss Willie B. Thomas, because I had heard that she was ill. She told me what medicine she was taking, and I told her everything I knew about that medicine I'd learned in my pharmacology classes. She smiled and seemed so pleased and said, in some surprise, "Why, Henry, that's just exactly what the doctors told me too."

She was taking digitalis, and was delighted with my erudition on the subject. I told her jokingly that now that I was becoming a doctor, I could teach her a few things, kind of evening the score between us a little. In some detail, I regaled her with the history of digitalis. In England, someone had noticed that cows grazing in a certain field were getting sick and dying, but in a nearby field other cows were just fine. They switched the cows from one field to the other, and saw that the cows that weren't sick started to die and the ones that were sick got better. A flower in the field, a purple foxglove, was responsible for the cows' good health, and thus the medicinal properties of digitalis became known.

I was probably a terrific bore, full of myself and my new knowledge, but Miss Thomas listened with what looked to me like rapt attention and pleasure. She said she just loved it that I was going to do something constructive with my life, and she could see I was growing up fine. Her praise meant a lot to me, and it made me feel good that I could give her a little something back.

The warmth that I felt in my home community dissipated as

soon as I returned to the university, where I was very aware of how separated I was from the other students, and not only socially. My differentness was brought into especially sharp focus one day during clinical pathology class, where we had been studying various blood abnormalities. In preparation for the class, the reading assignment included a section on sickle-cell disease, which I had really not known about before coming to medical school. It registered in my mind, of course, that this condition affected one out of twelve black people, but I hadn't somehow considered myself at risk. I knew I didn't have the disease because I had none of the symptoms, so the reading seemed academic.

As part of the clinical class work, we were told to prepare a glass slide with a drop of our own blood for examination under a microscope. The way it was done required that we use a chemical compound that took a minute to cause the blood cells to change. All at once it occurred to me that there might be more at stake for me here than a simple class lesson on blood; I was about to discover if I carried the trait or not, and suddenly the assignment was personally meaningful for me, in a way that it couldn't be for any of my classmates.

That minute took a very long time. Waiting for it to pass, I looked around the room, and as I picked my eyes up from the slide, I saw that ninety-five other pairs of eyes were staring in my direction. As soon as our eyes made contact, everyone got busy with their microscopes. I knew that they had realized, just as I had a moment before, that something important was at stake for me and they were watching to see my reaction to my blood slide.

Very reluctantly I focused the microscope and the flood of relief that coursed through me when my cells didn't sickle taught me something about how stigmatizing it feels to have a genetic defect. I knew I was simply lucky, and as grateful as I was, I decided that I would learn much more about this terrible disease and see if I could improve the outlook for those who had it.

My social isolation in medical school was in some sense counteracted by the embrace of the African-American community in Little Rock. The town's physicians, especially, realized that the few black students in the school needed support, and consequently they treated us like extended family. They invited us to barbecues and celebrated holidays with us, and generally made sure that we knew that we were really not entirely alone—as we so often felt. Through their kindness and generosity, I began to realize what tremendous resources for involvement reside within a local community, and in later years tapped this awareness to good advantage.

But it was a very lonely time, and I missed my family and friends. My father came for one of his rare visits to me after I'd successfully completed my first term in medical school, and I could see how proud he was of what I had accomplished. As a way of symbolically marking my coming of age, for the first time in my life he took me out for a beer. I recognized this rite of passage for what it was, and I was very moved by the way this undemonstrative man was able to demonstrate that he thought of me as an equal, or a buddy, someone grown up, a man.

Soon after this visit, my father died. I was in the middle of a physiology lab when a technician came in to say that I had an important telephone call from my sister in Pine Bluff. Clearly, something was terribly wrong. I raced to the phone and said, "What happened to Mother?"

She said, "It's Daddy," and then nothing else.

My father was dead. He had been working at the arsenal and suddenly fell over where he stood. Possibly it was a heart attack or an aneurysm; we were never sure, because we didn't have an autopsy. The African-American students, all six of them, took time off from school to accompany me to the funeral because they thought I should have their support. None of the other students did. I have been grateful to Sam Kountz, Delmare Edwards, Willie Mott, Earl Clay, Ernest Burnell, and Henry Cooper all these years.

My father had taught in Pine Bluff at Merrill High School, the public school for blacks, for so many years and had been the athletic coach for such a long time that he was very well known, and highly regarded, in the community. It was an impressive funeral. Many of his former students were in attendance and a few spoke publicly about what an important influence he had been in their lives. They told of how his confidence in them had motivated them to attempt goals they might otherwise have ignored and about how his striving for excellence had pushed them to aim higher too.

I was very sad; but there was little time for mourning. I had to get back to my studies. In some way, as a kind of tribute to my father, I worked myself even harder after his death. Through some kind of magical alchemy, I thought that if I was tremendously successful, he would be pleased. I realize now that this was my way of grieving, but at that time I thought that my accomplishments were an offering, a gift to him, my way of saying good-bye and of thanking him for believing in me.

After my father died, many people were extremely kind to me. I remember how impressed I was when a complete stranger offered me a job one summer at the urging of my good friend Sonny Walker. Sonny and I had grown up together, and he had played football on my father's high school team. He was very aware of how much I missed my father; I think he might have missed him too.

That summer, Sonny and I had planned to work in Indianapolis together. He had gone on ahead of me because his college vacation began before medical school let out for the year. He was working as a waiter at a country club and happened to overhear a man and his daughter arguing about the name of one of the characters in a Shakespeare play. Sonny was an English literature major and knew the answer; excusing himself for intruding, he told them who the character was.

The man was impressed, and asked Sonny about himself. He explained that he was a college student working as a waiter for the summer. They chatted for a while and then Sonny said that he had a friend, a medical student at the University of Arkansas, the only black student in the class, whose father just died and who needed a job. Sonny, as well as knowing Shakespeare, knew how to present a good case for what he wanted. The man turned out to be the president of the Monarch Buick Company; he gave Sonny his card and told him to tell me to come see him so that he could give me a job.

When I arrived in town I did just that. The receptionist was not particularly pleased to see me, and in a most perfunctory way told me to write down my name and wait my turn. I told her that I knew that the president of the company really wanted to talk to me, and showed her the card he had given Sonny for me. Most reluctantly she called him and told him I was there; he ushered me right into his office and offered me a job as a driver of company vehicles.

We became friends. At the end of the summer, when I was leaving to return to school, because he knew how eager I was to own a car, he arranged for me to buy a terrific Chieftain Pontiac, with a mere 6,000 miles on it, at a wonderful price. When I graduated from medical school, I sent him an invitation to the graduation ceremony. His kindness and friendship meant a lot to me.

My time in medical school, the 1950s, coincided with the beginning of the civil rights movement in the United States. The armed forces had been integrated by President Truman's executive order, and in Montgomery, Alabama, in 1955, Rosa Parks had refused to get up and go to the back of the bus. Reverend Martin Luther King, Jr., was establishing his philosophy of nonviolent social action, and prejudice was becoming untenable to many people; segregation did not seem natural as it had in former times. The doctors at the University of Arkansas Medical School were affected by these changes as much as everyone else, to my great advantage.

When I was rotating through surgery, a couple of my fellow students came to me, irritated, and asked me why I wasn't carrying my load of patients. I had no idea what they were talking about and went to the chairman of the department, Dr. James Growdon, so that he could look into the situation. We went together to the secretary who wrote up the lists, and he asked her, "Why is it that Foster has no patients assigned to him?" She answered, "We never assign white female patients to black students."

To his credit, and my immense relief, Dr. Growdon became furious with her. He asked her to accompany him back to his office, where he sat her down and very emphatically told her that there was to be no such policy, in fact there had never been such a policy, and that if she had assigned patients on this basis in the past, it was to change from that moment on. Did she understand? Every student was to be treated equally; race was irrelevant; and he was never to hear about her making decisions and calling them school policy again. She said, "Yessir, yessir, yessir," and after that walked a wide circle around me.

My determination to succeed was rewarded when I was nominated for the most prestigious academic honor a medical student can achieve, Alpha Omega Alpha, considered to be the Phi Beta Kappa of medicine. In the fifty or so years of the honor I was Arkansas's first black student to receive it, and of course I was immensely pleased, both to have gotten the scholastic recognition that the award marked and also to find myself on the top of a crumbling barrier. Other black students would be better accepted in the future.

It was only many years later that I discovered there had been several faculty members who'd attempted to block my nomination, arguing that the time wasn't yet right to integrate the AOA. Thankfully there were enough others who thought my work merited this honor and protested against this thinly veiled bigotry, in particular, a young professor involved in the process, Kermit Krantz, who threatened to expose the university if they blocked what everyone knew was a deserved award. He'd threatened to go public, tell the newspapers, and show that the school was bigoted and practicing racial discrimination.

Today Krantz is one of the world's most respected teachers and researchers, a brilliant man who eventually became chairman of his department at the University of Kansas. Even more important, he proved himself to be a decent and brave person who wouldn't tolerate prejudice, and I received the honor. Our friendship continues to this day.

It was during my senior year in medical school that I had a firsthand look at the cavalier, and sometimes worse, way women can be treated by physicians, and I know that my thinking, and practice of medicine, was shaped by this experience. I was very involved in what was happening in the field of ob/gyn, and so when the Pap smear was introduced, I suggested that my mother go have this important screening test for cervical cancer. She took my recommendation and saw a doctor. After her appointment, she called to say that the doctor had scheduled her for a hysterectomy because he had discovered a fibroid tumor.

Even though I was only a student, I needed to assure myself that this was the correct treatment. I knew that fibroid tumors were generally benign and that they usually shrink during menopause, which my mother was approaching. A hysterectomy would be indicated only if the tumor was causing excessive bleeding or was very large. When I asked her how big it was, she said something like an orange. I didn't want my mother having any unnecessary surgery because I was not unmindful of the fact that at that time 1 out of 2,400 people died just from the anesthesia. I have always been conservative by nature, and remain so about potentially dangerous medical procedures.

I told my mother to call her doctor back and cancel the surgery until further notice, and then I arranged for her to come to the University of Arkansas Medical Center to see the chief of the ob/gyn service. To this day I remember perfectly what he said. After examining my mother, he told me not to worry because "these kinds of tumors are common in colored girls." My mother, the colored girl.

I have always been very good at keeping my emotions in check, especially when it would be stupid to let them fly, and I calmed down by reminding myself that this man was a product of his culture, he really didn't know any better. I asked myself what would be more useful to me, to get into a confrontation with him or to let him take care of my mother. The answer was obvious, so I quickly swallowed my upset and ignored his thoughtless remark. My mother didn't need surgery after all, and was later buried at the age of eighty-six with all of her organs intact. But this episode made me vow I would always be cautious about recommending medical procedures, and indeed in the following decades, I have prevented dozens and dozens of women from having unnecessary hysterectomies.

Racial tension was high in Little Rock, Arkansas, during the fall of 1957, which was final year in medical school. The integration of Central High School in Little Rock had become a rallying point for reinforcing the government's position against institutionalized discrimination. The U.S. Supreme Court had ruled unanimously several years previously, in 1954, that racial segregation in public schools was unconstitutional. The High Court had found that the system of "separate but equal" schools did not, after all, result in all students having equal access to educational opportunities—far from it. As a result of this decision, it was mandated that public schools become integrated.

Orval Faubus, then governor of Arkansas, decided to ignore the Supreme Court ruling; he was not in favor of integrated schools. Over his dead body, I think, was his opinion on the matter. Daisy Bates and others took up this challenge; they encouraged a group of black students to enroll in the all-white Central High School. Wiley Branton, my father's student in Pine Bluff and my first airplane ride partner, ended up being the attorney who brought suit against the Little Rock Board of Education on grounds they were operating against the law of the land. He represented a young student, Ernest Green, who along with eight others was courageous enough to defy Faubus and the system.

Governor Faubus called out the National Guard to prevent Ernest Green and his classmates from entering the high school. I will never forget the experience of seeing grown men, soldiers, holding bayonets at the backs of children, to keep them from getting an education in America, the stronghold of democracy in the modern world. Extraordinary photographs appeared on the front pages of newspapers in virtually every major city in the world, and all I knew was that America's hypocrisy could no longer continue, that this was certainly not America's finest hour.

President Eisenhower was no great champion of the civil rights of black people, I don't think, but he did understand the American Constitution, and he knew that the country had to honor its Supreme Court decisions, that Faubus could not simply decide that he and the state of Arkansas were above the law. In order to ensure that the constitutional rights of the students were upheld, the President was forced to federalize the Arkansas National Guard and send federal troops into Little Rock; armed, they escorted the nine children into the school.

I watched the federal troops, the 101st Airborne Screaming Eagles, come streaming across the Arkansas River, and stood in the street and cheered. One of my father's favorite quotes was from Frederick Douglass, and seeing the troops enter the city, I remembered it: "There is no growth without conflict." I was sure that this conflict would move the country toward more equality, and indeed "Little Rock" became synonymous, for a generation of people, with the fight for integration in the South.

When Ernest Green graduated from Central High, it was a celebrated event for proponents of the civil rights movement. Daisy Bates invited Dr. Martin Luther King, Jr., to come to Little Rock to mark the occasion, and because I was "visible," the only black student in my medical school class, and because I had myself broken a barrier with the AOA award, Daisy Bates asked me if I would greet Dr. King at the airport with her.

I was a great admirer of Dr. King and I was honored to be called upon to meet him. I respected his courage because I knew what Alabama was like; his house had been bombed, his life had been threatened. I thought he was a hero, a man taking chances to open up some closed doors. Sitting in Mrs. Bates's living room, we spoke about our mutual alma mater, Morehouse, and reminisced about teachers and fraternity life; we discussed his admiration for Gandhi and his policy of nonviolence. The hour passed quickly and then he was called away.

CHAPTER FOUR

Doctor, Please Help Me!

INTERNSHIP AND RESIDENCY

After graduating from medical school in 1958, I went to Detroit Receiving General Hospital, associated with Wayne State University, for my rotating internship. I chose Detroit because the hospital had a wonderful reputation and a highly regarded staff; also it was one of the busiest services in the country, delivering over 9,000 babies a year. I was pretty certain that I was going to specialize in ob/gyn because the breadth of expertise required appealed to me—internal medicine, endocrinology, nutrition, and surgery—and I knew that I would get a tremendous amount of experience working in Detroit.

Internship in those days was as much a test of endurance as anything else; we worked for twenty-four hours straight, sometimes longer, and then had twenty-four hours off. When we were on duty, there would be times when we were physically and mentally stretched to our limits. Years later, this grueling schedule was modified, and residency training became slightly less physically arduous, mostly due to a public outcry that arose after a young woman, Libby Zion, entered a New York City hospital and died. In the ensuing investigation, it became clear that her treatment had been compromised by the questionable care she'd received at the hands of the exhausted residents and interns.

With my demanding schedule, it was a most impractical time to fall in love, but I suppose everything indeed has a season, and my first year of internship was mine. I had a blind date arranged by a good friend, Al Luck, whose room was right next door to mine in the dormitory. Al and I had a lot in common: he had been the only black student in his class at the University of Virginia, and we also drove the same model car—1958 Chevy Impalas—and therefore became known as the Impala Twins. When he told me he knew someone he wanted me to meet, I was automatically interested.

St. Clair Anderson, he told me, was a friend of his from Howard University who was working nearby as a nurse in the Dearborn VA hospital. I arranged to take Sandy, as she was called, to a Halloween party. She lived in the nurses' residence, and when she came down to the lobby that night I wanted to run right back to my dorm—to kiss Al Luck. Sandy was wonderful.

I thought of myself as too much of a serious scientist to actually believe in love at first sight, so I decided that my attraction was the result of pheromones gone wild. Regardless of what I told myself, I knew I was smitten, and I worried terribly that Sandy would never be attracted to me. Happily she was. We had a splendid time at the party; we laughed; we liked each other and after a few months of dating we were inseparable. We always said we met by Luck; Al enjoyed the pun as much as we did.

In addition to these new relationships, I had the pleasure of meeting up with my friend from Morehouse, Don Moore, who was also doing his rotating internship at Detroit Receiving. He had gone to Meharry for medical school after college and we had lost touch. Now we were on similar career paths, as we both planned to continue with our residencies in ob/gyn in Detroit, if we were accepted into the program.

The chairman of the ob/gyn department, Dr. Charles Stevenson, was an unusually farseeing man; he had publicly vowed that he wanted to increase the number of minorities in his training programs so that the population that was being served would be reflected by the staff. Over 95 percent of the patients were black, and over 90 percent of the staff was white. Dr. Stevenson was determined to enlist good minority doctors into his program, and encouraged both Don and me to apply. This was an unusual program in that it required its ob/gyn residents to have a full year of general surgery residency before beginning ob/gyn residency training. I liked the idea of more training; it made sense and I was excited to participate in this unique program.

Don and I both got accepted, but before we could break out the champagne, we each discovered that we had been drafted into the military. All doctors were expected to serve two years in the armed services; under the Berry Plan there was a lottery for when that service would take place, either after internship or after completion of residency. Temporarily shelving my year of surgery, I became a captain in the Air Force, while Don went into the Navy and was sent to Japan. Once again our paths parted.

I wasn't going to let the Air Force interfere with my emotional life, however, and Sandy and I became engaged, planning to get married the following year while I was still in the service. For some doctors, doing military service disrupts their training; for me, just the opposite occurred. It seems I was in the right place at precisely the right time.

Just as I was preparing to leave for basic training, I received a communication from the Air Force saying that they had a shortage of doctors with ob/gyn training. From my credentials, they had noted that I might have such an interest, and now wondered if I would be willing to spend three months doing an intensive course in ob/gyn at Carswell Air Force Base near Fort Worth, Texas. I would then go on to my permanent assignment, where I would work exclusively with a civilian ob/gyn consultant. It was exactly what I would have asked for had I had the choice, and it didn't take me long to tell them that I was the man for the job.

At Carswell I worked one-on-one with Dr. Morissey, who, in a short while, trusted my facility enough to let me handle most minor procedures by myself. I became quite expert. On the more complicated cases, I assisted him, and soon developed a great deal of technical and medical skill. I was lucky to have such an intense immersion in hands-on procedures, which was the equivalent of a private residency.

When I finally got to my permanent assignment in the state of Washington, I practiced with a marvelous man, Dr. Anson Hughes, who was a board-certified obstetrician in the city of Moses Lake. After about a year together, Dr. Hughes stopped coming into the office altogether, unless I called him with an emergency. All told, I managed to deliver almost five hundred babies while I was in the Air Force.

There were very few black doctors practicing in Washington, and my presence there took getting used to for some people. One of my patients, the wife of a base commander, came to me with a gynecological problem and articulated what must have been in several of my patients' minds. After three or four visits, she was very comfortable with me, and said, "Dr. Foster, I'm going to tell you something and I hope you won't misinterpret me. I really like coming to you," she said, "but I must admit that when I came the first time I had some reservations. I had never in my life been to a black physician."

I told her I knew just exactly what she was feeling because until I had come into the Air Force, I had never in my life been to a white physician. I think people forget that these roads go in two directions.

Busy as I was in the medical practice, I was also making plans for Sandy's and my wedding. As the date, February 6, 1960, approached, I had to get myself across the country, from Washington State to Washington, D.C., Sandy's hometown, where we were to be married in the Salem Baptist Church. In the Air Force the way one travels is to go to flight operations at the base and find out which planes are flying where, and if space is available, hop on one of them. I was lucky to find transport with Ray Shauer, who was conveniently flying to Florida, which was at least on the same coast as Sandy.

We had quite a trip. First we stopped at Mather Air Force Base at Sacramento, California, to load a Minuteman missile, a solid-fuel rocket, which we delivered to Cape Canaveral, Florida. On the way, we encountered some terrible thunderstorms over Alabama. At night, a blue bolt of lightning struck the plane and there was a surge of electricity that went from the nose to the tail in a flash. I felt the hair on my arm stand on end; and the idea crossed my mind that Sandy was going to have a slightly toasted groom at the wedding. When we landed, we saw that some of the plastic had been blasted off the radar dome of the plane. The wedding was unaffected by this near miss and soon Sandy and I were back in Washington together, having taken a commercial propeller plane, as decidedly happy newlyweds.

During my second year in the Air Force, I received a letter from Dr. Stevenson asking me if I was still planning to enter the Detroit program, and if so, where was I planning to do my compulsory year of surgical training. He recommended a few places which he thought were superior, and I chose Malden Hospital in Boston, Massachusetts.

To get there on time for the beginning of the term, Sandy and I drove fifty-nine hours nonstop from Washington to Boston. We finally pulled up to the hospital at two-thirty in the morning, dropping with fatigue. The hospital had a doorbell, which I thought quaint, and I rang it hoping someone would let us in at that hour. In a few moments, a creature in green scrubs appeared at the door, and above the mask I was surprised to see the laughing eyes of Don Moore. Once again, we had followed the same path without knowing it; from Japan he had determined to do his surgical residency in Malden too. He had discovered my name on the list of new residents and arranged to be our welcoming committee. Having a friend in this new situation, and in this exclusively white enclave of the Northeast, made us both feel a little less isolated.

Our first baby, Myrna Fay, was born during our stay in Boston, and I can remember the joke I made when I brought her home. Malden, like Dearborn, Michigan, had no black residents. The North gave some lip service to being more liberal and integrated than the South, but these noble intentions didn't extend to housing communities, which were racially restricted.

When we were ready to bring our daughter home, I called all the nurses and the staff together in the nursery and told them that they were about to witness something extremely rare in American society. "You will see one of the great advantages of being an African-American. Look around, everybody. I am the only father in Malden who can be absolutely positive that he is bringing home the right baby." There was only one tiny brown face among the sea of white ones.

It has been my experience that underlining a point with humor is more effective than with polemic, and I hoped to suggest to the staff that this lily-white population might not reflect everyone in the country, including their own black residents.

Although the year at Malden was interesting, I was eager to get back to Detroit and continue with the residency program in ob/gyn. Just as Don and I were beginning to make our plans, we heard troubling rumors that Detroit Receiving was having administrative problems and there was some question about its continuing accreditation. We discovered that the program was indeed in difficulty and thought to be somewhat unstable, and we were advised to think about doing our residencies elsewhere.

This left us in a very awkward position, because it was late in the year to be applying for residencies, but that is exactly what Don and I had to do if we wanted to go anywhere other than Detroit. I spoke to the chief of surgery at Malden, Dr. Walter Garry, and asked his advice. He strongly encouraged me to apply to a teaching hospital, rather than a private one, and I agreed.

Don and I both decided to apply to Meharry because of its superlative program in ob/gyn. We got lucky; they accepted only two residents that year, and they took us. It seems we owed this decision to a Dr. Philip Nicholas, who was on the staff at Meharry and saw our applications. He thought our records superior because we had had much more experience than the students who were coming directly from medical school. We had both worked for two years in the service in addition to the year of surgical training in Boston, and this put us a total of three years ahead of our competition.

Furthermore, we both had fine credentials. I had won the AOA in medical school, and Don was already a highly regarded technical surgeon. Our colleagues used to say we made a perfect team: I was the brain, and Don was the hands. Dr. Nicholas convinced the chairman, Dr. Walter James, that our experience would enhance the standing of the department, and so, as late as it was to be applying, we were accepted.

I found out the hard way that coming into a new situation required more social finesse than I was used to. Shortly after I arrived at Meharry, we were having a patient review meeting, discussing the case of a woman who had a blood-clotting abnormality. I thought her treatment somewhat archaic and said so in no uncertain terms. What I said was that I had just come from Boston and people were using a much more advanced treatment for this condition, and we should adopt the new approach for the welfare of the patient.

Dr. James, chairman of the department, got upset that this new young resident was telling him his business, and Dr. Nicholas had to pull me off to the side and tell me to be quiet and let him handle the situation. It took him a few moments to calm Dr. James down, but he convinced him that such "new bright blood" was exactly what the staff needed. I tried to be more circumspect after that.

Other staff members were not thrilled to have two young hotshot residents enter the program either, mostly because they were worried that we might be too big for our britches, especially me, with my academic record. They weren't exactly gunning for us as we arrived, but we did feel that we should watch our backs.

One of the instructors, whom I came to respect highly, Dr. Charles McGruder, had decided to make it clear that I was not such a know-it-all as my records, and my attitude, might indicate. I knew he was looking to bring me down a peg or two in front of the other staff members, so when he asked me to diagnose a certain patient, I was on my toes.

In front of several people, he had me examine a woman and then asked me to tell everyone what I found. During my Air Force experience I had done thousands of pelvic exams, and I suspected McGruder would not be questioning me about a straightforward situation, so I was especially cautious about the diagnosis. After examining her, I told McGruder that I thought I knew what her condition was, and acknowledging the waiting audience, I said that I was pretty sure that the patient had a bicornate or double uterus. I was correct, and he was not pleased, but he managed to sputter out, "I'll be damned, he got it," before he marched away. It was so apparent to the others that he had hoped to embarrass me that his plan backfired; and I think everyone but Mcgruder was happy with the way my "test" worked out.

There was another incident, early in my training at Meharry, that increased my reputation for being a good diagnostician, and for being someone who would not kowtow to superiors. As I was walking through the ward one day, a woman who was not my patient pulled on my sleeve and said with some desperation, "Doctor, help me. No one around here believes what I tell them. They keep saying I put something in my vagina, but I never did. And I keep telling them, but no one will believe me."

Something in her expression made me sure that she was telling the truth and I promised to come back to her after I had finished my rounds. When I returned, I saw that her chart said she was being treated for chemical burns of the vagina, a condition commonly associated with criminally corrupt abortions. The scam went something like this: A woman would be prepped for an abortion. Then the "doctor" would place potassium permanganate, a highly caustic element, into the woman's vagina; bleeding would ensue and the woman would believe that she was indeed aborting. What was actually happening, however, was that the blood was flowing from the burnt vagina, not from the uterus. By the time the woman realized that she had been tricked—and badly injured— the crook would be long gone with her money, and the devastated woman would require hospitalization. Since no one could ever admit to having participated in this procedure, abortion being illegal at the time, women were forced to lie about the cause of their injuries, so it was not unusual for a woman to swear that nothing had happened to her—and for her not to be believed.

But I was convinced that this woman was telling the truth. On examination it became obvious that her condition could not have been caused by a chemical burn, because she did not have what are called "kissing" ulcers, sores that were in exact opposition to each other, which occurred when the vaginal walls collapsed. What she had were peculiar purple lesions on her cervix and vagina, which in no way resembled a chemical burn.

No one had taken the trouble either to examine her carefully or to listen to her pleas, and I was angry at the callous way this poor woman had been treated. What's worse, I thought I knew what was the matter with her; I thought she was suffering from a fatal kind of cancer, choriocarcinoma.

This rare condition is a malignancy of the placenta, and when I looked up her records, I found that she had had a miscarriage the previous June, so it was likely that my diagnosis was correct. I wasn't subtle about letting everyone know that I thought the staff had ignored both the person and the symptoms. In fact, I told the chief resident that he had "bungled" this case, that nothing in this woman's physical condition or history suggested a chemical burn, and recommended that he get chest X rays and do a biopsy, both of which unfortunately confirmed my diagnosis.

Although the chief was not pleased to have a new resident tell him his business, and show him to be in the wrong, I thought Mrs. Brown's treatment warranted risking his displeasure. The staff doctors, on the other hand, were impressed both with the subtle diagnosis and with my nerve in confronting my chief. The nurses liked what I had done also. I would like to think that the residents were more careful with their patients, and perhaps kinder too, after this episode.

By far, the best part of the residency at Meharry was the six months we spent at Tuskegee. Tuskegee, Alabama, is one of the poorest parts of America, very much at the lowest end of the economic totem pole. It is also the site of the historic Tuskegee Institute, established in 1881, as a place committed to the education of southern blacks. As depressed and impoverished as the surrounding rural area was, the Institute itself had an impressive history and was an island of progressive education. Booker T. Washington was the first principal of the school, and George Washington Carver used the campus library for his agricultural research. Tuskegee is the place to go if you want to know about black history in the United States; here, for example, is the repository of the records of all the racial lynchings that have occurred in this country.

The John A. Andrew Memorial Hospital at the Tuskegee Institute was the center of medical care for the poor black people of Alabama. Delivering medical services to this community was a tremendous challenge because the rural population was suspicious of doctors, and of medicine in general, and preferred not to have anything to do with us. Women almost universally had their babies by themselves, or with the help of lay midwives. Prenatal care was virtually nonexistent and infant mortality was high.

When a birth was uneventful, we wouldn't hear about it, a case of dog bites man, but if the woman was in crisis, bleeding or in obstructed labor, or had a ruptured uterus, or some other medical catastrophe, someone would bring her to the hospital. Therefore, almost everything we saw was an emergency, and in a short time we had been exposed to more pathology than would be found in a more sophisticated urban community. To an eager resident, it afforded a look at "high-need" medical care in its most dramatic form.

I was thrilled to be working in such a high-need environment because I knew that I was truly making a difference in people's lives, often even saving their lives. These women needed medical care desperately and I almost as desperately wanted to make an impact on health care in the region. As engrossed as I was in the work, however, there was a downside, which was that I could see my family only once a month. I was in Tuskegee when our second child, Wendell, was born, or, more accurately, I was on a train frantically trying to arrive in Nashville in time for the birth—without success.

The commitment of members of the medical community to improve the lives of the rural poor was inspiring. On the staff of the John Andrew Hospital were Dr. Eugene Dibble, the medical director; Dr. Joe Mitchell, chief of ob/gyn; Dr. Tom Calhoun, chief of surgery; Dr. Tom Campbell, chief of pediatrics; Dr. Calvin Dowe, chief of medicine; Dr. John Hume, chief of orthopedic surgery; Louis Rabb, hospital administrator; and others. Some doctors came from Emory University in Georgia to help supervise our training, simply because they knew help was needed. One such doctor, John Daniel Thompson, became my mentor. Like my father, he was not a man who openly communicated his affection, but after I passed my specialty boards for certification in ob/gyn with a very high score, I overheard him bragging that I was his favorite resident.

I was beginning to acquire a reputation for taking chances and being right. Also, I could make things happen in a way that impressed the staff, little things really. For instance, the room where we scrubbed to get ready for surgery was very poorly lighted, which seemed idiotic to me, and an easy problem to solve. I collected some money and had fluorescent lights installed so we could see what we were doing. I remember that Dr. Thompson thought this remarkably innovative.

Just as had happened in the Air Force, I found myself in the right place at a needy time. Within a few days of finishing my third-year residency rotation, the chief of ob/gyn, Dr. Joseph Mitchell, tragically died. The medical director of the hospital, Dr. Eugene Dibble, needed someone to cover and he asked Don and me, as the chief ob/gyn residents, if we would fill in until a new chief could be appointed. Don and I alternated every other month and managed to do the job. After several months I received a call from Dr. Dibble, who informed me that the board of trustees had decided to offer me the job of chief of ob/gyn at the John A. Andrew Memorial Hospital. Would I accept? I hadn't even finished with my residency, I reminded him, but he said he was well aware of that, and the position, if I wanted it, would be waiting for me when I finished.

I wanted it very much, and accepted.

PART II

THE FOLKS THAT AMERICA FORGOT

CHAPTER FIVE

There Has to Be a Better Way

TUSKEGEE

The decision to take up the post at Tuskegee was easy for me to make; I knew I would be doing work that was critically needed, highly valued, absorbing, and important. For Sandy, however, it was not as immediately attractive, because she was concerned about how our two young children would fare in this impoverished and depressed rural region. We talked about it at length and eventually she became convinced that the family could overcome whatever sacrifices would be required.

The need for a well-trained ob/gyn in Tuskegee was immense, and neither of us, as committed health-care workers, could bear to turn our backs on this seemingly forgotten portion of America. The deprivation in the area was heartbreaking, and we weren't going to walk away from it; we weren't going to disappear, like so many other people, into a middle-class void and pretend it wasn't there.

I had originally been attracted to a specialty in ob/gyn because of the intellectual challenges involved; but working in Tuskegee I became aware of how the lack of maternal and child care in this region resulted in massive health problems. Babies were dying, by and large unnecessarily, and this was simply unacceptable to me. It became obvious that there was a critically important relationship between social problems—poverty, in this case—and medical care.

The plight of these poor, mostly black families was nothing short of intolerable, and Sandy and I were united in our disgust with a system which seemed impervious to their condition. Decades earlier, my mother had helped poor rural women with their nutritional needs; now, in 1965, I was determined to improve the health care of a similar population.

I accepted the position of chief of ob/gyn at the John A. Andrew Memorial Hospital and my family prepared to move to Tuskegee. Although I could have earned a great deal more money in another location, when Dr. John Thompson had recommended me for the job, he had insisted that the Institute pay me a decent wage, so we knew we would be able to manage. The house that we were building was not quite ready for occupancy, so we moved in with my Aunt Sadie and Uncle Bailey, my mother's oldest brother, who was the head of the agricultural extension service at Tuskegee Institute. Although we were somewhat disappointed not to be in our own home, living as part of an extended family for a short period of time made the transition to our new life less stressful. I'm sure having us with them was work for my aunt and uncle, but they were wonderfully gracious, even when Wendell, our infant son, stood up in his crib and tore down Sadie's lovely curtains.

Now, if only I could have just as easily reached out and pulled down the barriers to health care, the work wouldn't have been so daunting. As the sole obstetrician in the area, I was the doctor responsible for providing care to the women of Tuskegee, and eight surrounding counties. There were very few doctors of any specialty practicing in this impoverished area, and almost no African-American ones.

Rural women took for granted that they would have their babies at home, perhaps with the help of lay midwives. Their attitude toward their own health and that of their families was fatalistic; they believed whatever happened was meant to happen, and so they had little inclination to seek out any form of medical intervention. Many of the poor rural black women of Alabama had never been to a doctor in their lives, and those who did require medical care ran the risk of shameful treatment by the many white doctors who relegated them to small closets in their offices, away from the front rooms, where the white patients awaited service. It was common practice at that time that, no matter what the emergency was, no matter how urgent, black patients were expected to wait until every white patient had been attended to. Only then would the doctor see them, and often in a most cursory and humiliating way.

Because they had almost no prenatal care, these women were often vulnerable to problems which might easily have been avoided. Frequently routine, relatively minor problems remained untreated, and they escalated until they exploded into full-blown emergencies; the women would be brought to the hospital half dead, in critical condition. It wasn't only local women who used our services; women from all over the state and beyond arrived at our door because there was no other place for them to go. No other hospital would accept patients who couldn't pay their bills, who were indigent, or who were in tremendous need of intensive care and costly treatment. Not surprisingly, the infant mortality rate in the region was high.

Clearly, some changes had to be made, some form of intervention was needed to prevent these needless deaths, so I rolled up my sleeves and got to work. I was assisted by a most experienced and highly trained nurse, Thelma Walker Brown, who several years later completed her Ph.D. degree. Thelma was bright, absolutely dedicated, idealistic, and not in the least impressed with my credentials. The day we met, I was in the emergency room running in ten different directions and shouting instructions. She walked in, took one look at me, and said I looked much too young to be the doctor in charge. I assured her that I was older than I looked, and she responded, "That's good, because you don't look more than ten years old." We liked each other immediately.

Unlike several of the doctors I had been with in school who treated the nurses as if they were their servants, I was perfectly aware of how dependent I was on the staff. The nurses knew where the forceps were kept; I didn't. But I knew enough about what I didn't know to align myself with as many people as I could. Thelma and I became a very good team, and together we tried to staunch the flow of crises that poured through the hospital doors.

She had worked with obstetrical patients for many years before coming to Tuskegee, and yet her wealth of experience had not prepared her for the emergencies that were our daily fare. For example, pre-eclampsia and eclampsia are among the most serious complications of pregnancy and in fact can be fatal, but these conditions can be easily controlled through regular blood pressure screening. In most areas in this country, eclampsia is so rare that a doctor can go for years without treating a single case, but since there was such a lack of prenatal care for the poor rural women in Tuskegee, and certainly no blood-pressure monitoring, this condition was commonplace. In fact, we had so many women with eclampsia coming to the hospital that we quickly established a protocol for effectively handling this emergency.

Thankfully, our work resulted in some success stories too, or we might have become overwhelmed by the constant level of crisis management. One Saturday morning I found myself with a patient who was the wife of one of the senior vice presidents of the Tuskegee Institute. Marian Torrence told me, when I asked how I could help her, that she was pregnant but needed to terminate the pregnancy because she was unable to carry to term. She had had eight previous pregnancies without a success because, as she explained, she had an incompetent cervix which dilated prematurely and caused her to go into labor before the fetus was viable. The foremost reproductive endocrinologist in the world at that time, Dr. Greenblatt, had treated her during her last three pregnancies and hadn't been able to stop the problem from occurring.

A few years earlier, an East Indian doctor, Dr. Shirodkar, had devised a procedure for just this situation; although it had been applied before, I recommended it to her again, telling her that it had a 50 percent chance of success. The drawback was that she would have to spend a great deal of time off her feet and in the hospital. She thought the effort worth it and decided she wanted very much to try again.

I also treated her with a drug called Vasodialin, which was then thought to dilate blood vessels and increase blood flow to the uterus. Fifteen years later, however, it was found that this very drug worked by inhibiting uterine muscle contractions, exactly what the doctor would have ordered if the doctor had known at the time. I had good instincts on this case, and even better luck.

After she got completely stir-crazy from being on her back in a hospital bed for months, Mrs. Torrence begged me to let her go home, promising that she would stay in bed. I made regular house calls and watched her progress. When she did go into labor, she had a critical emergency, which I was able to take care of. Her lovely daughter, Andrea, was born without undue complications.

Regardless of whether the work was rewarding, I knew that unless we made some profound changes in the health care of this region, we would be spending our time applying Band-Aids to hemorrhages. The entire system needed to be overhauled; the question was how to do it. One of my first orders of business was to make it clear that every single patient would be treated with dignity and respect, regardless of her financial, educational, or social status. Early in my tenure at Tuskegee, I found an opportunity to let the community know that I was really there to serve them—all of them.

I had been called to the hospital in the middle of the night because two patients had been admitted with problems; one, the wife of a vice president of Tuskegee, had a minor ailment, and the other, a very poor rural woman, was suffering from an emergency condition called placenta previa. Of course, I took care of the emergency first. This incident must have been a subject of conversation, because a few days later a hospital administrator came to me and said, "Hank, people are saying you can't tell the private patients from the clinical ones."

I answered, "You're absolutely correct, and as long as I'm chief, no one else will either." I insisted that people be seen on the basis of medical priority only.

Changing attitudes was only a first step; what was urgently needed was money to extend existing care and make it more accessible and effective. The previous Washington administration, under President Kennedy, had been generous with federal funds, especially for the medical care of babies, and money was still flowing from the Title V Children's Bureau during the Johnson years. Grants were available—the Maternity and Infant Care Projects, as they were called—which would support a program that could demonstrate through innovative means an improvement in the health care of mothers and infants. This was exactly the opportunity we needed at Tuskegee and we determined to apply for one of these government grants.

The first step was to design an innovative proposal that would impress the government officials and convince them that under the proposed program the region's infant mortality rate would decrease. But before we could write such a proposal, I thought that I needed a better handle on what I called the Big Picture in medical care. My sense was that we had to concentrate on preventive care rather than crisis management, which only made good sense to me: if we could stop problems from occurring at the outset, we wouldn't have to resolve them when they became emergencies. So I took myself to the library to learn something about the sociology of medicine and health-care delivery.

Tuskegee Institute had an excellent sociology department and I read every spare minute I could. In the 1960s, it was unusual to think about the epidemiology of medical problems, but unusual methods were indicated. I was convinced that unless we broke new ground, we would stay forever mired in an inadequate and unused health-care system. The sociology texts alerted me to problems that were beyond the scope of my medical books: I learned about attitudinal and organizational barriers to health care, nonmedical issues that might prevent people from being the beneficiaries of even those systems that were designed to help them.

We had superlative services available to women at the John Andrew Hospital; that wasn't the problem. It wasn't enough, for example, to be able to treat eclampsia successfully. We wanted to try to reduce the number of people who needed emergency services, and I wanted to figure out a way to get the people who did need those services into the hospital before a serious condition erupted.

Furthermore, because of the terrible way poor black women had traditionally been treated by the medical establishment, I knew that care had to be delivered in a user-friendly way. Many patients felt like captives to a medical system that was difficult to negotiate and rigidly impersonal. Even as a resident I had always hated it when I heard people referred to as "the ruptured appendix in bed three" or the "C-section," because I knew no one wanted to be spoken about that way. I had no hard evidence, but it had been my experience that people healed better when they liked and trusted the people who cared for them, as if their immune system responded to kindness and concern. After a surgical procedure or a delivery I always tried to call my patient and ask about their well-being, after they'd left the hospital, not because I wanted to be a nice guy, but because it was a successful medical technique.

I also thought that if we looked at the delivery systems of health services—the "organizational aspects," as the sociologists called them—we would be able to improve care. Vaccines were available to children, but they were only valuable if the children actually received them. You don't have to be a rocket scientist, or even a cocky young obstetrician, to realize that if people have no access to medical care, they won't get it. It was simple really: We had to find a way of bringing medical services to the women who needed them. But putting a system in place didn't in itself guarantee that the region's women were going to embrace it, especially considering that they had no experience with health care, no understanding of what we could offer, and a great deal of ambivalence toward people in positions of authority. Our goal was to find a way to reach them, physically and psychologically.

A team of people—health-care workers, nurses, social workers, nutritionists, a pediatrician, and I—thought and thought and thought and finally developed a workable idea. The remarkably simple, practical, obvious, and innovative solution was: Take our services directly to the people who needed them. Go into the community rather than wait for them to come to us. If we brought a team of health-care workers into the outlying districts where the women lived, and helped and educated them, we would eventually win their confidence. By gaining access to them, we could offer a full range of health-care services: prenatal care, nutritional counseling, pediatric support, social services if necessary, and postnatal and infant care training, and contraception. We would be able to monitor conditions like hypertension, diabetes, heart disease, etc., and so improve their overall health. If we could introduce the idea of comprehensive, holistic, and preventive care to this population, many of the medical crises typical of this region might be avoided.

So far, so good; but now we had to devise a way to actually implement an outreach program of the proportions we envisioned. The people we hoped to treat were spread over a large geographic region, and our facilities for treatment were few and far between. We realized that if we integrated the different parts of the system into a single, unified, regionalized concept, we would be able to use the existing facilities in a novel and most practical way.

A regionalized health-care system is based on the premise that there should be an interaction among different levels of health care for a specified geographic area. Assume that a region has a population of about a million people, and a birth rate of 15 births per 1,000 per year. That makes 15,000 births in that region. Approximately 20 percent of the pregnancy population can be expected to require the most sophisticated services available—that is, about 3,000 patients will have serious complications and need specialized medical attention, half of which could be diagnosed during the prenatal period.

If we used the John Andrew Memorial Hospital as the top-level, or tertiary-care, facility for these patients, and the outlying clinics as secondary-care facilities where routine examinations and non-emergencies could be handled, then everyone in the region would have access to an appropriate level of care.

We had some highly skilled doctors usually available to us—urologists, orthopedists, ophthalmologists, etc.—because those who were on staff at the VA hospital in Tuskegee were also consultants to the John Andrew Hospital staff, and we could enlist them when necessary. Moreover, we would use the John Andrew Hospital as the site for continuing medical education in the region and also as a research center, collecting and analyzing data on the epidemiology of what were successful interventions and what needed more research and development.

Our proposal, painstakingly written, outlined how we planned to provide comprehensive medical care for a large geographic region by assigning specific uses to different facilities. Through prenatal screening, we would be able to identify and triage those patients we suspected would require hospitalization and special services. Holistic and preventive health-care information and services would be offered in the outreach clinics. Our proposal also addressed more practical issues—for example, how we would resolve the transportation problems typical of poor rural areas, given that there was no public transportation in the region and many people couldn't afford cars. How could women get access to care even if they sought it out? If we went out to them, then the problem was resolved.

Our overarching hope was to change patient attitudes; we wanted to convince these mothers that their health mattered. If we could demonstrate that we were committed to them, then maybe they would begin to take their own health care more seriously, which in turn would mean their babies would stand a much better chance of surviving the first years of life without serious, avoidable illnesses.

There were fifty-six Maternity and Infant Care grants awarded nationally, only three in rural areas, and we at Tuskegee were the recipients of one of them. This meant we now had sufficient funding for health-care workers, nursing staff, transportation, and hospital services; our regionalized health-care system was underway.

Not before we ironed out some unforeseen wrinkles, however. Making use of the outlying clinics as regional care facilities had some unanticipated problems; many of them were in such appallingly primitive condition as to be useless. One, a virtual out-house, collapsed around us as we worked. In winter, the clinics were so cold that neighbors had to arrive before we did in order to light fires in potbelly stoves; otherwise the rooms would not be warm enough for the women to undress to be examined. In summer, there were other problems. Once someone bumped into a wasps' nest while I was examining a patient and the wasps swarmed all over us, which was unsettling for everyone, especially the patient. Somehow we managed.

The women who came to us appreciated the seriousness with which we approached their health care and their comfort. In summer, in the terrific Alabama heat, our team would arrive with ice water in big jugs, and our patients relished the cool drinks as if they'd been offered a rare treat. We didn't realize it at first, but in fact this was exactly the case. Fresh drinking water was not always available in these districts and some people had to travel miles every day just to bring back water for the family's drinking, cooking, or bathing. As simple a pleasure as a cold drink of water on a summer day made a clinic visit something of value.

No one who thought himself superior to this unsophisticated population worked with me for long; there simply wasn't any room in our project for a team member who had an "attitude." The women we saw had rarely been treated with dignity, by doctors or anyone else in authority, which was unforgivable. They certainly hadn't chosen to be impoverished, and I expected everyone to treat our patients with great respect. I never referred to my patients, some of them old enough to be my mother, as Mary or Susan, as so many of my colleagues did; it was always Mrs. So-and-So, and it was obvious that they were surprised and very pleased to be spoken to in this way.

Adequate staff was another problem; there just weren't enough hands to go around. As the only obstetrician/gynecologist at the hospital, I was constantly on duty, working around the clock. Not only did I make weekly visits to the outreach clinics, but I had a large office practice as well. I saw private patients during the day-time hours when it was convenient for them to come in, and the clinic patients at night when their workday was over and they had time. The students at the college also needed medical services and had to be fit in somewhere in-between. They had no money to pay, yet didn't have the proper profile to be admitted as clinic patients, so I saw them privately and didn't charge them. If they had some access to sound medical advice before they needed obstetrical care, everyone would benefit in the long run. In addition to all this office work, I was delivering babies day and night and handling emer-gencies. There was simply no way to be "off duty" and in Tuskegee at the same time.

I worked so many hours that I hardly saw my family. One day I arrived home and found Sandy working under a large tower of books. "What's this all about?" I asked her.

She said. "You're working twenty-four hours a day, and might have a heart attack any minute. I have kids to raise."

She had decided that her R.N. degree wasn't enough and she wanted to pursue a B.S. degree. I wasn't sure whether she really thought that I would collapse from overwork, or whether she'd simply decided to take advantage of being in a college community, but whatever the reason, Sandy went back to school and, to no one's surprise, least of all mine, was the ranking graduate in her class.

It was clear that I needed some assistance to do this very demanding and time-consuming job, and I thought I had the per-fect idea. Our health-care program had shown me the benefits of using existing resources in novel ways and I knew where there was a ready supply of helping hands. I wrote a long letter to Dr. Walter Fitz Burnell James, who had been my chief when I had been a resi-dent at Meharry, proposing a student rotation in ob/gyn at Tuskegee. If we could have the third-year medical students for a few weeks, we could teach them something invaluable about rural health care, obstetrics/gynecology, and high-need medicine. They would get wonderful experience, and I would have a few extra peo-ple to take blood pressure and do histories and physicals.

I can remember what I wrote: "It is academically unresourceful to share this volume and breadth of clinical material with only a single resident physician." How could Dr. James resist such rhetoric? He wrote back and listed about a dozen matters that would have to be resolved before such a program could be implemented: where would the students live, who would supervise them, how would we document their work, etc. As quickly as I could, I responded to every one of these issues, and by October our first students arrived.

They came directly out of the classroom into what must have seemed a war zone, but the energy and the enthusiasm of the Tuskegee medical community was infectious, and they all did just fine. We wanted them to feel good about being with us, which they did. It didn't hurt any that Sandy invited each group of students for dinner at our home. I was especially pleased that so many of the students who worked with us eventually decided to specialize in obstetrics and in the process became sensitive to the importance of preventive health care.

It seemed that every time we managed to plug up one hole in the dike, another one would sprout. Once the personnel situation was improved, we had to deal with transporting patients to different facilities. Although we were using our outreach clinics to evaluate our patients, a percentage of them needed hospital care, which meant they needed some way to get to the hospital. Again, there were unlikely resources at hand in the form of hearses.

Undertaking is a surprisingly good business in terribly depressed areas. When you are as poor as the people of Tuskegee, you just *know* that the afterlife will be a better place than this one, and virtually everyone had a burial policy and believed in fancy funerals that would send them along in style. I befriended the local undertakers, most of whom had hearses available which were sitting idle much of the time, and told them, "Your clients aren't going anywhere. They're going to be right where you left them when you come back. They can wait. Mine can't." In this way we acquired emergency ambulances and drivers.

We also had to find a mechanism to cope with the flow of information involved in treating people in different facilities. Accurate records of histories and treatment were needed for each patient who moved through our system. There were no computers, but there was an adequate substitute—carbon paper. Every woman who came to see us came away with a document chronicling her medical condition; that paper, which some could barely read, was her ticket into the hospital when she went into labor or if an emergency arose. This simple solution kept our patient information remarkably accurate and up to date.

By far, our biggest hurdle was overcoming the patients' attitudes about health care, so we looked to people in the community for assistance. We were able to locate a practical nurse at the hospital, Mrs. Bellman, who was eager to do something to improve the lives of the rural women who were having twelve and fifteen babies. As she succinctly put it: "That just can't be good for them." Indeed not. She and a cadre of women like her, active in the church and well known in the community, traveled into the rural areas and taught the local women about contraception, nutrition, and general health care. They also encouraged women to come to the clinics for regular examinations and Pap smears. Our goal, in the satellite clinics, was to educate our patients about preventive care.

There were some surprising health advantages to bringing care directly into our patients' home environment. For instance, when babies were delivered in the hospital, the nurses would teach new mothers how to make enough formula for a day of feeding. Breastfeeding, which we encouraged, was frequently insufficient to meet the infant's needs because the mother's nutrition was itself inadequate; therefore supplementary formula feedings were often required. The hospital nurses had no way of knowing that many women had no refrigeration at home, and babies were getting sick from ingesting spoiled formula. As soon as we identified the problem, during follow-up home visits it was a simple matter to teach the mother how to make the formula one bottle at a time, and the situation improved.

Integral to our holistic approach to preventive health care and patient education was making contraception available to the women who wanted it. IUDs were especially popular because at that time it was the only form of contraception that could not be discontinued passively; an active decision was required to get the device removed. Also, I used Depo-Provera, a drug which had been on the market for several years in this country but had not been approved for birth control by the FDA—for all kinds of political and foolish reasons—even though it was routinely prescribed for contraception in over ninety other countries around the world. Although it is perfectly legal to use a drug that has been approved for one purpose for another, the doctor who does so risks malpractice litigation.

Politics sometimes gets in the way of good common sense in medicine. I knew this drug to be especially suited to the women I was treating and I was determined to offer it to them. Depo-Provera is of great benefit to people with sickle-cell disease because, unlike the typical oral contraceptive, it does not contain any estrogen. Sickle-cell disease sufferers are particularly prone to forming clots, and estrogen increases the risk of this. The drug was also extremely easy to administer, requiring only four annual injections, a real advantage in an area where transportation is a hardship.

In order to dispense this method of birth control to the patients who wanted it, I developed my own informed-consent form. I never knew of a patient who became pregnant while on this medication and no one ever sued me for malpractice. Even before the fiasco of the Senate hearings on my nomination for Surgeon General, I knew from firsthand experience that politics and medicine sometimes have different agendas.

Nonetheless, I learned how critically politics affects health care. Each year, I went to the Alabama State Health Office in an attempt to get increased funding for our clinics, and each year the director of the State Health Department, Dr. Ira Meyers, told me, "Look how much more money we're allocating for your clinics. Look how much better the black patients will be this year compared to last year." Then I would say, "That's fine. But when are we going to eliminate the gap between what white people get and what we get?" Slowly, especially after the people in Washington began to use our outreach program as a model for foreign visitors to admire, the gap began to close.

The director of the Children's Bureau during this time, Dr. Art Lesser, was a staunch champion of the Tuskegee program. He was impressed with its unique approach, in particular how we were going out into the community trying to do something that hadn't been done before. Our program was so successful that Dr. Lesser brought visiting health officials from developing countries to view what he touted as the quintessential model for rural health care. For all kinds of reasons, not the least of which was preventive care during the prenatal period, infant mortality had decreased greatly in this region under our program.

My overloaded work schedule provided me with just the excuse I needed to take up flying again. The value of such an enterprise was brought home to me one weekend when I was searching for someone to cover my practice for a few hours so that Sandy and I could attend an affair in Atlanta with our good friends Tim Boddie, a retired Air Force general, and his wife, Mattye. It was only a three-hour drive and we were all looking forward to having a night out, but as luck would have it, a woman was brought into the hospital with a complication which required my immediate attention, and after I finished taking care of her, it was too late to start out for Atlanta. We were all terribly disappointed.

Then Tim had an idea. He said that Chief Charles Anderson, a former instructor of the famous Tuskegee Airmen, taught ROTC for the Air Force at the college and owned two planes. Perhaps he would let us borrow one of them for the evening. I thought this an inspired idea. Chief was happy to accommodate us, and the trip to Atlanta took a mere forty-five minutes. Having a plane of my own, I realized, would make life easier and more pleasant for me and my family, and with little trouble I convinced myself that I should have one. I was busy; Tuskegee was isolated; Chief Anderson could help me hone my skills—all good reasons, for sure. The biggest reason for getting my own plane was that I had always loved flying and I missed it.

Chief Anderson was a most interesting person, and I was pleased to become acquainted with him. He was a self-made man, or, rather, a self-made pilot, which is indeed a feat. He'd taught himself how to fly an airplane when he worked for several years as a lineman at an airstrip where he had access to an old airplane. He would take it out, taxi it, then take it a little bit off the ground, and land it, repeating these maneuvers until he had a sense of mastery and felt in control. It is not an easy thing to do, to teach yourself how to fly a plane, but he was so proficient at it that he became a teacher of others. In fact, it was said that he could fly a plane with only one wing, a high accolade indeed.

I had grown up with the highest regard for the Tuskegee Airmen, and it was thrilling to me that I would have the opportunity to learn from one of their teachers. Chief's lessons were utterly practical and simple and I was an apt student. One of the first times I went up with him, he taught me something that, although perfectly obvious, not everyone is able to articulate. He said, "Hank, let me tell you something. If you see an object in front of you, and the top of it is below the horizon, that means you're above it. If the top of the object is above the horizon, you're below it—and where the horizon bisects this object is where you're going to hit it if you don't change your course." Chief Anderson also had the distinction of being the first African-American in this country to have an air transport license.

In 1970 I bought my plane, a beautiful brand-new Cessna Cardinal 177B, which I flew with great pleasure for twenty-one years. Sandy, although not nearly as enthusiastic as I was, didn't mind, and the plane offered our family traveling opportunities which would otherwise have been impossible. Shortly after I got back into flying, I took the family to a meeting in Atlanta and we met Don Moore and his wife, Barbara, there. Barbara asked Sandy how she had the nerve to fly in a small plane, especially with the children, and Sandy responded very simply, "We're all together." I don't think I would have enjoyed it so much if Sandy were unhappy or nervous about it.

Which is not to say there weren't times when nervousness was appropriate. Soon after I got the plane—the paint wasn't even seasoned yet—Chief and his wife, Gert, and Sandy and I were going to attend a meeting of the Negro Airmen International in Barbados, a trip we had been anticipating with pleasure. I was flying us down to Barbados, 3,000 miles from Tuskegee one way, and Chief and I had spent the four or five nights preceding the trip working on the charts and maps necessary for safe flying. In the Caribbean they didn't have the kind of sophisticated high-frequency navigation system that we have in this country, but used a low-frequency air direction finder, which made navigation much more difficult.

The flight began uneventfully, but after refueling in the Caicos Islands, the drama began. As we flew over the northern shore of Hispaniola, the island which houses Haiti on one end and the Dominican Republic on the other, we approached a range of mountains towering over 10,000 feet. Just then I heard some Spanish on the radio and responded with my best *"No español."* Fairly quickly a P-51D Mustang fighter plane appeared, very close to us, matching our speed and altitude, with the pilot gesturing at us to land the plane. I looked down and saw an airstrip far below.

I had no idea what was going on, but I didn't think I liked it, so I opened up the Foreign International Range frequency on the radio and said, "This is November 30820," which were my identifying call numbers. "I believe I am being forced down by Dominican fighter pilots." Then I gave my location and landed. There was a lot of activity on the ground; military people with guns were waiting for us. It was so hot in the plane that I opened the door but otherwise we all sat there without budging. A senior-appearing officer with a lot of metal across his chest came over and stared at me. I stared back without any expression on my face and tried not to break eye contact, a technique I had not used since Pine Bluff.

Finally, this little game of chicken resolved in my favor, and he broke away, kicked at the tire of my plane, and came back to the door. He asked me, "Why do you fly over our military field?" I pointed upward and said something about mountains and thunderstorms. He said he had to search our airplane; I said go right ahead. I certainly had no intention of arguing with this guy. Gert, who knew a little Spanish, was attempting to talk to him, but we quickly discouraged her, convinced that one misplaced vowel would get us all shot.

The military people escorted us off the plane and into a room, where people went through all our luggage very thoroughly and unpleasantly. Eventually the officer came in and apologized; he explained that we had chosen a very bad time to fly over, because they had just had trouble with Haitian refugees fleeing Papa Doc Duvalier and he assumed that we had been trying to smuggle people out. Now that he saw that we had no such intention, we were free to go. While all this was going on, night had fallen, and I was not going to attempt to fly over the mountains in the dark. I said I wanted to wait until the next day to leave. The Dominican military put us up in a hotel for the night and we had a marvelous dinner at their expense.

We arrived at our meeting in Barbados without any further difficulty, and when Chief and I walked in, late, to the room where the conference was being held, there was a tremendous burst of applause and cheering. It seems that the radio call with my location and situation had been picked up by an Eastern Airlines commercial pilot flying between New York City and San Juan; he had alerted the American Embassy in Santo Domingo, and they had made inquiries about our safety and notified the people in Barbados. We were big celebrities that day.

In addition to providing travel opportunities for me and my family, the plane was very useful for medical emergencies. I was able to go into rural Mississippi to consult on various cases or perform operations, which time constraints would never have permitted without the airplane. The plane also gave me more freedom to have some fun while on call. Once I had followed the Tuskegee football team to a game in Florida and there was an emergency at the hospital; someone was in grave trouble. They located me at the game, and while I was in the air, I was able to give instructions to the air traffic controllers, who then coordinated with the people on the ground. As soon as I landed, there was a car ready to rush me to the operating room.

I could also extend the range of travel for medical meetings because of the plane; these meetings were most useful, and the more of them my staff and I could attend, the better for the program. Once Thelma and I had a meeting to go to in Jackson, Mississippi, and I had no time to drive, so I offered her a ride. She was nervous about it and was absolutely positive that her husband, Drew, wouldn't want her to fly. He had told her he was confident that I was a fine doctor, but he had no idea about how good a pilot I was, and he didn't believe in taking chances. So Thelma thought she would drive herself to the meeting and see me there.

As it turned out, the day of the meeting was cloudless and fine, and Thelma changed her mind. She didn't mention it to Drew, who she thought would be none the wiser since we were expected home before dark, but she told her son where she was going, and said he needn't mention it to Drew. We had such a good time in Mississippi that we stayed much longer than we expected, and when Thelma finally arrived home, her son and Drew were sitting on the steps with their heads in their hands, looking like Norman Rockwell caricatures of misery, with the phone next to them. Drew said he was just waiting for the call telling them Thelma had been in a plane crash and was in critical condition. She promised never to ride with me again, and seeing how frightened he had been, never did.

It was Thelma who came to me one day with a brilliant and original idea that influenced health care throughout Alabama. Her neighbor, a Mr. Davis, worked in the VA hospital as a medical technician doing testing for sickle-cell anemia. Thelma realized how useful for genetic counseling it would be for us to identify potential carriers of sickle-cell disease before they conceived. Also, if we could identify babies born with sickle-cell disease, we could begin early intervention which would make a difference in the length and quality of their lives.

Mr. Davis explained that screening required only a simple blood test. For some reason very few health centers in the country were doing the screening or knew the procedure. Eager to do it, we immediately began offering sickle-cell screening as part of our Maternal and Infant Care Program. Because we were such a visible program and because Thelma had worked with people in the State Health Department, the word spread and health officials from around the country became aware of the screening. They came to Tuskegee and we showed them our simple procedure of drawing blood and taking it to the VA hospital for analysis. Now every at-risk baby born in the state of Alabama is tested for sickle cell.

Knowledge about sickle-cell disease was new in the 1960s, and unfortunately, as with many new medical discoveries, misinformation and confusion were rampant. In California, an insurance company had canceled the health insurance of those African-Americans who had the trait, not the disease, and there was some talk about the military not allowing people with the trait to serve. Obviously, the African-American community was going to suffer as a result of poor medical information.

Individuals who have the sickle-cell trait have no significant ill effects; having the trait does not in any way compromise the carrier's health. It is only when both parents have the gene that the offspring may inherit the disease. I realized that people were confusing the trait with the illness, and I knew I was in a position to provide the kind of information which might help avert this confusion.

I made it my business to talk to the state agencies and to whatever groups and individuals I could about the implications involved in distinguishing the trait from the disease. My role in Tuskegee, and my being a highly qualified African-American physician, gave my position strength, and I used whatever skills I had to relieve the anxiety of blacks who were as frightened as the insurance companies. The effort was successful; no one in Alabama lost their insurance, and I think the information I was able to give people educated them to good end.

Also, my work with sickle-cell diagnoses made clear the importance of genetic screening and counseling. Parents needed to know if they both carried the trait and thus risked bringing a child into the world with the disease. It was the doctors' job, especially the ob/gyn's, to make sure the parents knew the attendant risks. Then, if they did choose to have a child, and that child was born with sickle-cell disease, as doctors we would be able to introduce appropriate medical care as early as possible. With treatment, some of the more terrible complications and symptoms of the disease can be avoided.

More and more in the course of my medical career I saw the way politics seemed to affect the quality of health care, politics as well as the attitudes and prejudices of people who held powerful positions. We had just built a huge new hospital at Tuskegee with federal Hill-Burton funds when several white doctors in the area asked the city to allocate funds to construct another hospital. Why? Because, according to them, their white patients didn't want to come to the John Andrew Hospital because they didn't feel comfortable. One doctor in particular, Luther McRae, led the fight for funds. I didn't think this thinly veiled racism should cost the community money, and as president of the Macon County Medical Society I went to court to contest the plan. This was a poor community, and tax dollars were needed to shore up other public institutions, like schools and social services. We were successful in blocking the venture, and McRae left town to practice elsewhere.

When I began my medical career I had no idea that I would be encountering racism among my peers or that so much of my time would be spent dealing with the politics of bringing health care to the people who needed it so badly, a condition I considered an offshoot of the institutionalized racism in this country. The more I worked with the larger issues, the more convinced I became that preventive care was a necessary part of the solution to the health-care problems facing the poor in this country—black and white.

When the Robert Wood Johnson Foundation approached me about being a member of a national advisory committee to help them formulate policy for a regionalized infant-care program, I was eager to participate. The Foundation knew that in order to lower the infant mortality rate and to increase the birth weight of premature babies so that their health would not be compromised, poor women had to be brought into the health-care system. Dr. Lesser had led them to me because the Tuskegee program was attempting to address just this issue. The Foundation people liked my concept of having high-quality care at a central location, with outreach centers to identify the patients at risk for complications. They put $20 million into this project and now every state in the country has a regionalized perinatal-health-care system. The Tuskegee program was a model for the entire nation.

The innovation of the Tuskegee program, and its success, brought me to the attention of the prestigious Institute of Medicine of the National Academy of Sciences. They elected me a member in 1972, one of the youngest doctors ever to be admitted. I was truly honored. One of the responsibilities of membership is to sit on national committees that research and evaluate what is new and important in medicine. My first project was to study the public health effect of legalized abortion, a very large study staffed by Sarah Brown, now director of the National Campaign to Prevent Teen Pregnancy, whose senior advisor I am for the President.

My committee work and my membership in the Institute gave me much more clout than I had had previously, which meant that I was in a better position to get things done. For some reason people seemed to pay more attention to me after I received this distinction, and I knew that I had better make sure that what I had to say was on target. I learned everything I could about the health-care issues of large and unchampioned populations, especially poor women and children. Formulating policy at the national level was a most effective way to improve the health situation of these groups.

My work with the Robert Wood Johnson Foundation and the committees associated with the Institute of Medicine made me increasingly attractive to other policy-making groups. I was invited to serve on many national committees, mostly those working to improve maternal and perinatal care. I learned quickly the effectiveness of political power plays. For instance, when I was chairing a national committee for Planned Parenthood, we decided to confront the Nestlé Company because we were disgusted with the way they were conducting an advertising campaign in poor and developing nations.

Nestlé was putting up billboards showing attractive, happy mothers giving formula to fat, beautiful babies. The not so subtle message was that the women should stop breast-feeding their children and buy formula instead. This was dangerous and even unscrupulous advice because many of the women lived in regions which had unsafe water supplies, and water was necessary for the preparation of the formula. Further, the mothers could little afford to spend what money they had buying formula, especially when there was no reason to do so. They certainly wouldn't benefit; the babies wouldn't benefit; the Nestlé Company would be the only beneficiary.

What could our organization do that would be effective against this big business? Nestlé is part of the Stouffer Corporation, which owns hotels, so Planned Parenthood, which has many meetings in hotels all over the country, began to boycott these hotels for our meeting sites. We cost Stouffer a pretty penny and attracted a lot of media attention. Like magic, the billboards disappeared.

These years were very fulfilling ones for me. I loved my work. What we'd done had made a real impact on the health care of the region, and on that of the whole country since our program was being replicated in other areas. From a personal point of view, my family had put down very sturdy roots in the area. Nonetheless, when in 1973 Meharry Medical College offered me the position of chairman of their department of obstetrics and gynecology, I accepted. Meharry had been one of the forerunners of primary care in the nation, and what I had done in Tuskegee was strictly primary care. They were interested in population-based medicine, and so was I. I liked the idea of training new doctors, most of them minority doctors, and of influencing generations of students, of bringing more students into obstetrics and gynecology. Meharry was one of the two medical schools I knew of that were committed to educating primarily African-Americans, and I was eager to be part of that process.

CHAPTER SIX

Never Duck a Challenge

MEHARRY

There is a moving story about the founding of Meharry that appeals to me, especially since it is true. In 1826, a sixteen-year-old white boy named Sam Meharry was hauling salt in his wagon when an axle broke and he became hopelessly mired in mud. He saw a light in the distance coming from a small cottage. When he got there, he discovered that it was the home of a black family. They took him in, fed him, gave him a bed for the night, and the next morning freed his wagon and repaired the axle for him. Sam was so grateful for this simple act of kindness and generosity that he promised them, as he was leaving, that if he ever became successful, he would return the favor by doing something to help African-Americans. He kept his promise. By 1876, Sam and his brothers had become very rich, and they donated the then unbelievable sum of $30,000 to Tennessee Central College to establish a school of medicine for newly freed men. And so one act of generosity led to a second, reciprocal act, each transcending racial barriers.

Meharry Medical College has been the training ground of almost 40 percent of the African-American physicians and dentists in the United States. I knew, when I accepted the appointment to become the chairman of Meharry's department of obstetrics and gynecology, that students who come from poor and underserved areas of the country are themselves most likely to return to work in such areas. Therefore, along with imprinting a new generation of doctors with my particular philosophy of "Health Promotion, Disease Prevention," by taking up the post in Meharry I knew I would be involved in the process of training doctors to serve the people who needed them most.

It was important to me to encourage physicians to practice in what I call "tier-two cities," places off the beaten track where medical services are scarce. For example, there was a time, around 1975, when over 90 percent of all the African-American doctors in Georgia practiced in Atlanta, although other regions in the state were in need of minority doctors also. I suggested that my residents set up their practices in Huntsville, Alabama, or Pritchard, Alabama, rather than in Birmingham or Montgomery, because it was necessary to distribute a higher standard of medicine more equally throughout a state. My experience at Tuskegee may have shown these doctors that I practiced what I preached.

Chairing a large department required a great deal of administrative savvy. I wanted the people who worked for me to feel that they "owned" whatever work they did, that they were responsible to themselves first and then to me. My staff had a great deal of latitude—enough rope to hang themselves, some of them said—so that they could do whatever they thought would advance their knowledge and careers. What I asked of them in return were annual reports which documented their goals and outlined what they hoped and planned to accomplish over time. I would compare these with what they actually did: how many grants did they procure, how many meetings did they attend, what committees did they serve on, what writings had they published and where. These annual reports helped the staff members evaluate whether they had indeed accomplished their own stated goals. It was the ploy of a shrewd boss, I thought, and it was also the right thing to do. I never told anyone how to behave; what they did or didn't do reflected on them. Generally my staff was happy with this procedure and it produced very good results.

The students who were accepted into the medical college were of top caliber. In the late 1960s and early 1970s, placement in medical schools was extremely competitive because these were the years of the Vietnam War, and many people who might have pursued other careers in science applied to medical school in order to avoid being drafted into the armed forces. Each place was highly coveted and we were able to attract superior students into the program. I supervised them very closely, not necessarily common practice among chiefs of departments, but I thought that having residents be primarily responsible for teaching students was not the most desirable practice. If the students had senior staff in the trenches with them, they would not only learn procedures and techniques from the most experienced people, but they would also learn, I hoped, something about a commitment to the education of others.

As department chair, I was responsible for developing and establishing a curriculum which would use the talents of the faculty in the best interests of the students. The staff physician who had attempted to put me in my place when I was a Meharry resident, Dr. McGruder, was still on staff and still effectively involved in training new residents and students. Together we devised what we considered to be a sophisticated course of study. Each staff physician gave lectures on his or her area of expertise. I always gave the introductory lecture on the epidemiology of pregnancy because I had observed how poorly schooled most doctors were in what I like to call the Big Picture.

When I became an examiner for the American Board of Obstetrics and Gynecology, I always asked the doctors if they knew how many babies were born in America in a year. Since these doctors were hoping to become board-certified in obstetrics and gynecology, I thought this was a reasonable inquiry. Interestingly, about one out of five had no idea—worse, had not thought to ask themselves the question—but I faulted the medical education system for this failure of knowledge rather than the candidate. This gap was an indictment of our system: someone could go through four years of medical school and then four more years of advanced residency training and not have any exposure to the epidemiology critical to one's own specialty. If I had anything to say about it—and I did—Meharry students would be better informed and not be limited by the tunnel vision so often prevalent in medical training.

In addition to the introductory lecture, I was responsible for the lectures on multiple gestation (twins, triplets, etc.), diabetes, teen pregnancy, sickle-cell disease, and health-care access. Most of these areas of specialization were outgrowths of the work I had done in Tuskegee, but my expertise on multiple gestation was rooted in a very different source. After my stint as a member of the Ob/Gyn Test Committee for the National Board of Medical Examiners, I became active on the Undergraduate Medical Education Committee for the Association of Professors of Gynecology and Obstetrics (APGO), an organization that represents the undergraduate ob/gyn interests in all the academic medical institutions in America. In 1993, I served as president of APGO. UMEC, as the committee is called, was the group responsible for outlining the behavioral objectives for medical students and exploring innovative teaching methods. We detailed what the students should know in order to be well rounded and able to pass the National Board of Medical Examiners.

Reviewing these objectives for the committee, I discovered that there was absolutely nothing written about multiple gestation, a subject of which I had made a special study when I was a resident. Surprised at this omission, I went to the committee chair, Benny Waxman, and informed him that nothing was written about this important topic. "Of course there is," he said, but when he looked for himself, he realized that I was correct. "I'll be damned," was his response before he looked up at me and said, "You'd better write it up then." So I did, which in turn prepared me to impart the most up-to-date information on the subject to my students.

By far, the great pleasure of academic medicine was in working with the students and teaching them how to analytically think through medical issues as they came up. "What if I were making a trip," I would ask each new group of ob/gyn students, "and I had traveled eight thousand miles. How would you evaluate the progress of the trip?"

The students would respond with intelligent questions: How did you travel? Did you go with anyone? How long did it take? Eventually someone would ask, "Where are you going?" and I would respond with praise because that was the crucial question. Unless you knew where you wanted to go, there was no point in making the trip.

Bench research, or basic research, though crucial, is not the goal of medicine, I would remind the students; it is a process. Bench research can develop miracle vaccines (the process) but is of no value for the 40 percent of unimmunized children. The goal of the process is that the children become immunized. Working in Tuskegee had taught me that good health care involves much more than medical techniques, even highly advanced ones. It requires an adequate delivery system, a sociological understanding of the particular population being treated, and an awareness of the causes of inadequate health care in that community. "Always look toward the Big Picture," I repeatedly admonished the class.

As a former member of the Ob/Gyn Test Committee for the National Board and an examiner for the American Board of Obstetrics and Gynecology, I was in a very good position to help my own students and residents prepare for their National Board and specialty certifying exams. To my resident physicians, I gave very general advice, but still it was crucial. I would ask them, "What do you think you have to do to be successful at your oral exams?" They would answer, "Know the information." I would say, "Of course. What else?" They would list all the obvious answers, and I would keep asking, "What else?" until, exasperated, they would start to say things like "Make sure my fingernails are clean." Finally, after they had expressed everything they thought they had to do to pass their exams, I told them that having the data at their clean fingertips was not enough. They had to convince the three examiners that they knew what was important, and that they understood the context in which the data were meaningful, or they wouldn't pass. Talk about the issues, I would tell the residents, not isolated facts. Don't wait to be prompted, but open the discussion of important issues yourself.

I wanted our students and residents to have absolute confidence in the medical education they were receiving. Toward this goal, I became a staunch advocate for changing Meharry's policy of not requiring students to take and pass the National Boards. Many schools throughout the country didn't insist on the National Boards, for a variety of reasons, not the least of which was that it was widely known and recognized that standardized tests like the National Boards were culturally biased against minorities. Even so, I was convinced that our students should be required to pass them.

I knew how easy it was for someone to be judged simply by race and, in the case of African-Americans, to be judged unfairly and with prejudice by members of the majority culture. I never wanted it to be assumed that a minority doctor who graduated from Meharry had anything less than a superb education, or that there was anything second rate about the medical standards of our graduates. On the contrary, it was important that our students have exactly the same credentials as, for instance, the students at Harvard Medical School. Instituting the requirement that our students pass the National Board exams at or above the national standards would, I hoped, discourage unfair and often racially biased judgments.

Although there was some opposition at Meharry to this new policy, I, with others, forced its acceptance. Once our students passed Part I of this exam, after the policy had been implemented, the most remarkable change occurred in them. It was as if they straightened their collective spines and threw their shoulders back and began to walk prouder and taller than they had before. When they themselves knew that they were being measured against the same standards as everyone else in the country—and still excelling—their pride surfaced. It was a compelling lesson: never sell yourself short, and never duck a challenge.

Our participation in the National Boards had the extra benefit of enabling me to monitor the areas in which our students were most and least knowledgeable. With this information we could then concentrate on improving our teaching in the deficient areas. As chair, and as the person who had the responsibility for making sure our students were well trained, I found it a welcome yardstick.

Watching the students move from the classroom into the delivery room and seeing the residents develop was exciting. I frequently flew my Cessna to Tuskegee to help with resident training there, quickly changing from flight jacket to white coat. On arrival at the John Andrew Hospital, I would illustrate whatever clinical procedure was relevant at the moment and question the students and the resident about symptoms and technique.

Every once in a while there would be a student whose interest would visibly spark, and I would fan it as much as possible. Terry Cole was one such student, standing out from the others because he was white, Jewish, and a Northerner, and, I suspected, having a hard time integrating himself into the Meharry community. My own isolation at the University of Arkansas was still too vivid for me not to have some compassion for his position, and I took him under my wing.

He was extremely bright and very engaged with ob/gyn; I could see he had a talent for it. For many of these students delivering babies marked the beginning of their clinical hands-on experience with patients. Usually until this point in a medical student's education, their training revolves around book learning and laboratory work. As chance would have it, the moment I arrived at the hospital for this particular rotation, a baby was being born, so I showed the students how to do an episiotomy repair. Terry's eyes were shining and I knew right then and there he was destined to become an obstetrician.

After the hospital rounds, I invited him for a ride in my plane, and he accepted with alacrity. As I do when I have an uninformed audience, I told him the story of the Tuskegee Airmen. This was the first time he had heard about them, and I don't know which I was happier about, teaching him clinical technique or telling him something about this little-known contribution that African-Americans have made to the history of our country. I also talked to Terry about my experiences at the University of Arkansas, and I could sense that this exchange meant a great deal to him. Racism, in any direction, is a terribly lonely experience.

It was racism and the legacy of segregation that forced Meharry to send its medical students to Tuskegee for the ob/gyn rotation in the first place, since the two publicly funded hospitals in Nashville excluded Meharry from training its students and residents there. It was especially difficult then, in the early 1970s, with the echoes of the civil rights marches in the South still very close in our minds, to not be doubly affected by the racism of the still segregated hospitals in Nashville.

Meharry had always provided care to the minority population of the city, but the volume of patients was comparatively low, due, in part, to the fact that Nashville's black population is small for a southern city. The economy of middle Tennessee didn't call for slaves, because the land was unsuitable for cotton growing. Thus, African-Americans only make up about 18 percent of the total population. Since the black population of Tuskegee was short on doctors, and the historically black medical students at Meharry were short on patients, the association was useful for both groups.

In some medical specialties numbers of patients are not as crucial as for others. If someone is suffering from heart disease, for instance, many students can learn from a single patient. But obstetrics and certain other surgical training are different and require a volume of patients. Each delivery or surgical procedure has its own set of issues and complications, and it is the job of the instructor to help the students gain enough clinical experience to be able to make proper judgments on a routine basis. The Tuskegee rotation offered the Meharry students the advantage of a large patient base from which to learn.

It was not always particularly convenient, however. One of my resident physicians was most unhappy to participate in the six-month rotation. She was an East Indian woman who came into my office with her husband and explained to me what a hardship it would be for her to leave her family in order to go to Tuskegee. It would be separating her from her culture, which was important to her, and she didn't feel that she should be forced to do it.

I told her that I appreciated her predicament but that she had to decide between two compelling forces: her responsibilities to her family and culture on the one hand and to her medical training on the other. She should think seriously about what she really wanted to do, I told her, and make her decision accordingly. Never would I suggest that she do anything that would jeopardize her family life.

I knew perfectly well that she had hoped I would waive the Tuskegee rotation, but I really believed it was necessary for doctors to evaluate their priorities and decide what was important to them, that this wasn't my responsibility but theirs, which is why in this case I'd deflected the entire conflict right back onto her. Within a week, she was at Tuskegee. Her experience there was excellent and she is now a board-certified ob/gyn practicing in nearby Kentucky.

The resident physicians weren't the only ones who had to disrupt their lives. I had to travel there on a monthly basis to teach and supervise, and this involved a six-hour drive from Nashville or a flight of about one hour and forty-five minutes. Flying was clearly my preferred mode of travel. I realized that in order to be sure that I could fly in a variety of weather conditions, I would have to get my instrument rating, the real "ticket" that every pilot needs for secure navigation, and to keep that rating current.

The advantage of living in an urban area presented itself to me almost as soon as I decided I needed this rating. Scanning the Sunday paper, I saw that an instrument ground school course was being offered by a local adult education school. The program was sponsored by Middle Tennessee State University, which has an aeronautical program, and the instructors were from the college faculty. Class was held for three hours every Thursday for a semester, and I never missed it, even if it meant rushing back from various meetings in order to arrive on time. I think the most difficult written exam I have ever had to take, and I have taken very many exams in my life, was the one for the instrument rating. My instructor was especially pleased that I passed on my first attempt; he didn't expect it, because I was one of the few students not associated with the aviation industry.

Weather avoidance instruments are safer and better than relying on one's eyes or listening to weather reports because they can inform the pilot exactly where the thunderstorms are located. I was generally an extremely cautious pilot—my kids called me the "big chicken" because I wouldn't fly in less than optimal circumstances—and I wanted as much information as I could get about flying conditions. A wonderful new piece of equipment had just been designed especially for single-engine airplanes, the Ryan storm scope, which accurately located the electrical activity of thunderstorms.

As soon as I could, I installed one in my plane. Since I lived in the southeastern part of the United States, home to frequent storms, such a device could literally be a lifesaver. With the instrument rating and the new equipment on board, I felt that I would be secure flying wherever I needed to go, and this included such airports as Atlanta's Hartsfield and Chicago's O'Hare.

Ironically, as the hospitals in Nashville remained entrenched in their policy of rejecting Meharry as a training site, the Association of American Medical Colleges was reviewing its policy and deciding that it was time to recommend that medical schools introduce some diversity into their staffs. Suddenly I was a very hot property, a well-qualified African-American doctor, and letters of recruitment for chairmanships in ob/gyn departments all over the country began to pour in, from people I knew and people I didn't. My former teacher and champion from my University of Arkansas days, Kermit Krantz, even wrote me a very appealing letter about coming to his school, Kansas, which was very flattering.

But I wasn't interested. I had come to Meharry because I wanted to help the school maintain its reputation for excellence, and to keep its name in the forefront of medical education. I was not about to leave now. Meharry, like Tuskegee, was where I was needed. I had completed my residency training at Meharry, and I believed wholeheartedly in its commitment to the preparation of primarily minority physicians and its desire to address the health problems that are disproportionately severe in minority communities. Meharry was exactly where I wanted and needed to be.

*   *   *

Consistent with my goal of having Meharry recognized as a preeminent academic medical institution, I realized that the more well known I was, and the more work I was engaged in on a national level, the more prestige would accrue to the school. I became active on as many boards and commissions as I could. In addition to being a member of the Ob/Gyn Test Committee for the National Board of Medical Examiners, and the UMEC committee of APGO, I sat on the Nashville Academy of Medicine's Ethics Committee, and numerous other commissions. I was invited to be on the editorial board of *Academic Medicine* (formerly the *Journal of Medical Education*) of the Association of American Medical Colleges, which is a huge organization representing all 125 medical schools of America.

I had been one of the featured speakers at the annual program for the Institute of Medicine on the medical issues associated with the treatment of the mentally infirm and I suspect it was at that time that I came to the attention of the federal government and was then appointed to the Ethics Advisory Board by HEW Secretary Joseph Califano. This highly prestigious and important organization evaluated the ethics of biomedical research, on the fetus, the embryo, everything; unfortunately it died from lack of funding when a new administration came to power in the 1980s.

In addition to being active in local and national medical groups, I sometimes had the opportunity to travel to foreign countries for medical consultations. A remarkable trip came my way in 1978 when Meharry sent me to Malawi to do an obstetrical health needs assessment for the government there. The President of Malawi, Hastings Kamuzu Banda, had received his medical training at Meharry, so the relations between the school and this newly independent African nation were very cordial. They became even more so when Dr. Banda attended the Meharry Centennial in 1976, and as he got off the plane, right there on the tarmac, greeted by Ray Blanton, the governor of Tennessee, Richard Fulton, the mayor of Nashville, and Lloyd Elam, the president of Meharry, he wrote out a check to Meharry for $1 million.

Dr. Banda's story is a fascinating one. He was born early in the century in what was until 1964 called Nyasaland, in southeastern Africa. As a very bright child he attended mission schools, where he learned to speak and write English proficiently. Legend has it that Banda walked to South Africa, and because he could speak English, found himself a very good job as a paymaster for a gold mine there. But he wanted to be a doctor, so he traveled to America on a tramp steamer. Once here, he enrolled in a historically black college in Ohio called Wilberforce and then went on to Meharry in the early 1930s for his medical degree. He left the United States and became a prominent surgeon in Sheffield, England, where he practiced for many years.

In about 1963, when the British were trying to hold together the Rhodesian Federation, they tried to force Nyasaland into the fray. But the leaders of Nyasaland wanted no part of the upheaval and sent for their most highly educated native son, Dr. Hastings Banda, to come home. When he did, he was declared President for Life of the newly formed nation of Malawi.

The British authorities jailed him because he would not go along with their crumbling colonialism; while he was in jail he had a great deal of time to contemplate the future of Malawi, and he conceptualized changing the location of the capital from Blantyre in the southern part of the country to Lilongwi in the middle. When the British freed him and the country became independent in 1964, he did just that. Although it was predicted that the new country would quickly flounder, in less than five years they were exporting pork to Scotland and their tea and coffee industries were robust. He ruled the country as if it were his personal fiefdom, and as I understand it, was quite surprised when he was ousted from office in 1994 when the first democratic elections were held.

When we went there, in 1978, all I knew was that the health care of the women in the country was woefully inadequate, and the administration was interested in doing something about it. I was glad to help. One would think that traveling from Tennessee to Africa would make the world seem very large, but when Sandy and

I walked into a beautiful resort in the Great Rift Valley at Lake Malawi, we were greeted by the voice of Kenny Rogers playing over the loudspeakers. We couldn't get over it; 8,000 miles from home, in Africa, and we were embraced by the long arms of Nashville.

Malawi was a poor rural nation, and I modeled my recommendations for improving health care on the regionalization system we had developed for Tuskegee. Access to medical services was as difficult for the women of Malawi as it had been for the people of Tuskegee before regionalization. Almost 97 percent of the babies being born in Malawi were delivered in the bush by lay midwives. There was no prenatal medical care and those patients who had medical emergencies had no services at their disposal.

The geographical configuration of the country was particularly well suited to a regionalized health-care system, for the country was long and narrow, with a major cities located in the north, the center, and the south. Each of these cities had a hospital, which, as part of a regionalized system, could manage the health problems for that region. To make matters even better, the country had excellent transportation facilities because there was a very well-developed agricultural extension system, which meant that patients could get to the clinics and hospitals.

As I have learned again and again, it is often advice other than medical that has the greatest impact on improving health care. One of the most important recommendations I made during this trip was to suggest that the government provide incentives, such as money, to encourage the local midwives to record birth certificates, so that there would be some data indicating what the child population would be for each year. Such information would mean that long-term plans for the next generation could be developed with some accuracy: for example, teachers could be trained and schools built accordingly.

Just as Sandy and I were preparing to leave Malawi, we received a surprise message at our hotel informing us that we were to have an audience with President Banda. Before long we found ourselves seated at one end of a huge dining table with Dr. Banda at the other.

We still had no real idea why we had been invited to see him; and somehow I didn't think it was the medical project. However, after exchanging a few pleasantries, the purpose of our visit became clear.

He said, "Dr. Foster, I see you come from Pine Bluff, Arkansas. When I was in medical school in Meharry, my roommate was from Pine Bluff. Do you happen to know what happened to Dr. Patillo?"

I was struck again by what a small world it is, to be sitting halfway around the world, with the president of an African country, casually discussing old friends from Pine Bluff. Unfortunately I don't think I told Dr. Banda what he wanted to hear: I had to tell him that I believed Dr. Patillo had died from tuberculosis shortly after graduating from medical school.

At the close of our interview, Dr. Banda said to one of his personal staff, "Give these nice people some money." For a moment, as I remembered the check on the tarmac, visions of riches danced in my head, but better sense prevailed, and I managed to say, "No. No, thank you." The staff member came over to us and whispered that one couldn't actually refuse the President's offer. Always a quick learner, I accepted, saying that I would spend the money buying lovely gifts from Malawi to take back to the United States.

Shortly after we returned to Tennessee, we learned that the president of Meharry was planning to retire. I knew how important leadership was and I took an active interest in who would replace him. A very good friend and college classmate from Morehouse who was a graduate of Meharry, Ezra Davidson, was championing David Satcher. I had met Dr. Satcher only briefly in the early 1970s when he was heading the Sickle Cell Research Center at Drew Medical School in Los Angeles and I was doing research in Tuskegee.

He was a marvelous candidate, I thought—a brilliant doctor, researcher, and administrator, with a national reputation for excellence. Furthermore he had graduated summa cum laude from Morehouse College, so I had confidence in his education. David had done an outstanding job of setting up a department of family medicine at Drew University in Los Angeles, which demonstrated his administrative abilities, and he was also a great proponent of primary care, which was entirely in keeping with Meharry's approach.

David's personal story was one of overcoming great odds, and I thought it might prove to be an inspiration to others. He was raised as a poor country boy from Anniston, Alabama. His parents had only a limited education, but they also had total integrity, which they had clearly instilled in David and his siblings. David had successfully completed the dual degree program at Case Western University, earning his Ph.D. in genetics along with his medical degree. He had the further distinction of having been elected into the prestigious Alpha Omega Alpha national honor society.

I knew he had talked to Meharry's search committee and was lukewarm about the idea of becoming a college president. From what I knew about David, I thought that if he understood more about Meharry, he would change his mind. A personal plea would be the best tack, I thought, and so I flew to Atlanta and met him at the airport, where I told him that the least he could do, before he made a decision, was to come and visit Meharry, see the school first-hand and its impact on the community.

Just as I'd hoped, the visit to Meharry convinced David that being its president was exactly what he wanted to do with his career. David had gone into medicine, he told me, because he wanted to bring health care to the people who needed it most, and the story of Meharry is precisely one of serving those who are most needy. Also of great importance to David was the knowledge that Meharry was training physicians who would practice in the neediest communities. David did become Meharry's president, and true to his beliefs, during his tenure he created the *Journal on Health Care for the Poor and Underserved,* the only such journal of its kind in the country.

David Satcher served as Meharry's president for eleven years. When he left, the staff gave him a goodbye send-off, and on that occasion he told us a poignant story. His mother had just passed away, and although she was supposed to have been very disoriented, the last thing she did before she died was to sit up in her hospital bed and tell whoever would listen about her son David, who had been so ill with whooping cough when he was only two years old that his family thought he would not recover. They were poor and unsophisticated people and they couldn't get him the best-quality medical care, which ironically was available very close by, at the Centers for Disease Control in Atlanta. Now, all these years later, David was leaving his position at Meharry to become the director of the very same Centers for Disease Control. Clearly, this accomplishment had penetrated even her extreme confusion; David's mother's last words were filled with extraordinary pride.

Between David's proficiency and my visibility on various national committees, Meharry became better known in the academic community. It was a coup for the school when the Robert Wood Johnson Foundation chose me to be the director of a $12 million project on consolidating health services for high-risk adolescents and thus Meharry Medical College became the coordinating site of this very large program and its administrative center. Not bad, I thought, for a small minority medical school.

The Foundation chose me to lead the project because we had worked together on issues of maternal and infant care, beginning with their interest in the Tuskegee regionalization plan. At that time, we had been able to show that regionalization had a positive impact on the high infant mortality rate through getting high-risk patients into prenatal care at early stages of the pregnancies. Something many people don't realize is that even today the United States ranks only nineteenth in infant mortality when compared with other nations in the industrialized world. I concluded that project, and since then I have been a consultant for the Foundation on a number of other projects, such as the Rural Infant Care Grant and the Healthy Futures Project, both concerned with improving the health care of mothers and children.

Working with the Robert Wood Johnson Foundation appealed to me because one of their goals has always been finding new ways to bring health services to vulnerable populations, infants and poor mothers in particular. Sometimes these programs showed the impact of changing the attitudes of physicians, as when we determined that doctors had to go to the rural patients in Tuskegee and not expect them to come to the doctors; other research programs showed the positive effects of collaborations between community-based medical practices and academic and hospital-based services, something Meharry had been engaged in for years.

I really had the feeling that the members of the Foundation were kindred spirits; many of the concepts and strategies they believed in and tested I found I believed in also, and so I was always happy to work with them.

Our collaboration was successful all around, and became even more so when I rushed late from my office for a meeting one day when several Foundation people had arrived to make a site visit. As I walked in the door, I suddenly squealed very loudly and hurled myself at one of the visitors. No doubt everyone in the room must have thought that I had suddenly lost my mind. Not at all. One of the Foundation staff was a childhood friend from Pine Bluff, Ruby Puryear Hearn, who I hadn't seen in nearly thirty years.

It was as if no time had passed, and while the group looked on indulgently, we reminisced and carried on as friends do when such coincidences occur. As a young girl, she had moved away from Pine Bluff and the college where our parents were faculty members, and we had lost touch. Now I discovered that she had gone on to Yale and earned a Ph.D. in biophysics. Remarkable, I thought, that we should have come by such different routes to work on the same issue, delivering better health services to mothers and infants.

I don't think there had ever been a nonwhite director of a large multi-site national project such as this one, and it wasn't lost on me that the Foundation people had approached me to lead the High-Risk Young People's Program partly because I managed to bridge two worlds, the nonwhite working-class minority community who used our services and the more mainstream academic and professional one of which I too was a member. Such a bridge was important if both the high-risk young people and the Foundation itself were to be well represented.

The purpose of the High-Risk Young People's Program was to investigate the effect of consolidating health-care services for adolescents. The Foundation had done research on death and disability for all Americans of all age groups over a twenty-year period, 1960–79, and found that death and disability had decreased about 19 percent for all other groups except those between fifteen and twenty-four, for whom the rate had actually increased by 10 percent. In looking further, we saw the increase was due to accidental death, traumatic death and injury, suicide, homicide, mental illness, teen pregnancy, sexually transmitted diseases, alcohol and substance abuse.

It was clear that social problems were at the heart of these health matters, and the Foundation soon realized that adolescents were a very needy and grossly unrepresented group. These adolescents often did not have any insurance coverage, and until the late 1970s there wasn't even a distinct medical specialty called adolescent medicine. Adolescents, if they wanted or needed care, had to hopscotch all over the medical and social service systems, and it was obvious, from the alarming number of young people at risk in this country, that whatever interventions were in place were dreadfully inadequate.

This grant would make a difference in all that, I thought. Finally, these kids, who fell so easily through the cracks of the system, who were poor and disproportionately not white, would have a powerful spotlight to attract some attention. I believed that with the clout of the prestigious Robert Wood Johnson Foundation behind this program, people would finally take notice of this terribly neglected area of health care. Even getting health-care providers to pay attention to the plight of these kids had been very difficult up until now, and we hoped our research would change that too.

Some of the ideas generated by the High-Risk Young People's Program illustrated what could be accomplished through sheer ingenuity and common sense. For example, at one of the sites, in Chicago, a powerful alderman named Danny Davis noted the foolishness of forcing schools within a very heterogeneous system to teach exactly the same health education curriculum in the same way to all students in the district. Some schools had a teenage pregnancy rate as high as 20 percent a year, while others had a rate as low as 5 percent. Still, the same approaches and services were being applied across the board. Davis realized that homogenizing everything for every school in a district, regardless of the particular needs of that student body, was highly ineffective, and that specific problems needed to be addressed on as local a level as was practical.

Julia Lear, my extremely competent deputy director, and I had hoped, as part of the grant, to introduce a teen pregnancy prevention clinic into one of the high-risk schools, but the school board was against this because they felt it singled out a particular school. But to us that was the point; it was that school in particular that needed the clinic. Alderman Davis was instrumental in convincing the reluctant school board to allow us to institute such a service, and as a result a clinic was set up and began to offer counseling and information about abstinence as well as contraceptive issues.

As director of this program, I found myself thinking more and more about what could improve the lives of the high-risk young people I saw all around me at home in Nashville. Then Leon Dash's report on teen pregnancy appeared in *The Washington Post*, and my ideas began to gel. Dash had gone undercover, living anonymously in a poor, high-crime area of Washington, D.C., in order to gather firsthand information on teenage pregnancy. His surprising discovery was that girls twelve, thirteen, and fourteen years old were actually trying to become pregnant. This was shocking information, and my feeling was that if a twelve-year-old girl sees nothing worthwhile in her life other than having a baby, it is our society that should be indicted, not the deprived young girl.

As I thought about it, I realized that merely having the capacity to prevent pregnancy is completely useless if there is no desire on the part of the people involved to prevent the pregnancy in the first place, a patently obvious idea but one that really hadn't been deeply considered. Why did these young girls want to have babies in the first place? Clearly, teenage pregnancy was as much a social problem as a medical one, and needed to be analyzed in as comprehensive a way as possible.

The High-Risk Young People's Program had shown that the location of social and medical services influenced the frequency with which patients took advantage of those services. Most programs aimed at the problems of teenagers were school-based, and there were certain built-in limitations as a result, especially having to do with the number of hours and days schools are open. In addition, many of the most troubled adolescents were not even in school, because they have dropped out of school, been expelled, or were truants.

What would be a more useful site? I decided to explore the impact of situating a multi-service program in a residential setting, a program that could be specifically tailored to Nashville's at-risk adolescents. Since by this time I had had some experience in getting funding for the implementation of new ideas, on behalf of Meharry we applied to the Carnegie Corporation, known for their interest in issues affecting young people, and received their support to develop what is now called the I Have a Future program, a service program with the goal of improving the lives of young people at high risk for failure. The name I Have a Future was suggested by Dr. June Dobbs Butts, who served as a consultant, and I thought it was the perfect moniker.

Unlike many such programs, the I Have a Future program was purposely designed to operate out of the public housing projects where these high-risk adolescents lived. This made perfect sense when we discovered through surveys and other means that most teenagers get pregnant between the hours of three in the afternoon and seven in the evening—the unchaperoned time after school, before parents come home. It would be very useful, I thought, to have a chance to work with the kids during these hours.

There would be many advantages to situating the program in the housing projects: it would be highly visible, and parents, siblings, and other community members could become involved too; and those adolescents who weren't in school would be able to participate in the program. If the services became part of the fabric of these kids' lives, in their faces all the time, as opposed to something outside their communities that they had to travel to during specific hours, we could reasonably expect to have more influence on their behavior and attitudes.

I know enough sociology to know that a population where 87 percent of the people earn less than $5,000 a year, which was the case in Nashville in 1987, and 92 percent earn less than $10,000 a year, is a high-risk population. Poverty breeds risk. Children are alone a great deal of the time because their parents—most often a female single parent—work long hours or are themselves suffering the consequences of poverty. The deck is stacked against these kids even before they take their first breath.

A friend of mine who is a psychiatrist once made an interesting point on this topic. He said that when kids grow up in rural squalor or urban slums, and really have nothing positive to look forward to, having a baby at an inappropriately early age is a sign of good mental health. Why wouldn't a poor and seriously deprived child want something to care about, like a baby who would find them crucially important and so on? Obviously, when you consider the problem of teenage pregnancy as a healthy response to an impoverished environment, providing condoms to kids is somewhat beside the point. The only way to improve the situation is to change the attitudes of these youngsters, to help them reconceive their futures in terms that hold some promise for a better life. This idea was the bedrock of our program.

Nashville, like so many other cities across America, had no shortage of poor, deprived, troubled adolescents, many of them living in public housing developments, and there was no shortage of places to locate our program. We chose two housing developments: John Henry Hale and Preston Taylor. Some of these kids had been told for so long that they were worthless and stupid and that they wouldn't amount to anything that they had begun to believe it themselves and were filled with despair and hopelessness.

This futile attitude was one we had to try to reverse. Never having had any instruction about how to wrestle with frustration, many of the kids didn't realize that in order to achieve success at something, they had to work at it. To them, it seemed that success was some kind of a natural attribute, like being short or bow-legged, and one that they themselves simply didn't have.

My mother had taught me an important lesson about education when I was in school which I passed on to the kids in the program. When, as a child, I would become impatient with having to study, she would say, "Brother, I don't care how smart you are, you cannot know that the Empire State Building is in New York City unless you see it, or read it, or someone tells you about it." I wanted to reassure these kids that their deficits had nothing to do with being stupid or incapable but were simply the consequences of a lack of exposure. And I promised them, and myself, that I would do all I could to offer them a wide variety of stimulating and creative experiences. With effort on their part, and with support from us, these kids could have many more options than otherwise.

Whenever I have a chance to speak to the kids in the program, I tell them exactly the same thing I tell my students, and what I told the East Indian resident who had to choose between her family and the responsibilities involved in the Tuskegee program. I tell them that they have their own minds and I have no intention of telling them what to do. But they need to evaluate the consequences of their choices. I tell them the facts: that a teenage mother has a very high risk of living in poverty for the rest of her life; about 70 percent do. Nobody wants to be poor, and postponing premature childbearing decreases the chance of living in poverty. I remind them that there are options open to them, especially if they stay in school. It's not necessary to have a baby as a teenager, I tell them, to have something of value in life.

Before we could devise a program suitable to the needs of the teenagers we hoped to service in Nashville, we had to learn something about them. I didn't want to go into these communities and dictate to the residents what I thought would be best for them and their children. Such an outsider stance and patronizing attitude would only breed hostility. We knew that in order for the program to be successful, the parents and the community had to support us, and so we needed to include their views in the design and conception of the program. To this end, we surveyed 497 heads of household and asked them to tell us what they wanted for their kids. Their responses were just the same as that of any parents: they wanted their children to live without crime, violence, teen pregnancy, sexually transmitted diseases, and to have job opportunities and training.

On the basis of these surveys, Dr. Chris Arthur, Michael D'Andre, Hagtib Zarit, and I developed services and programs that were designed to show these children that the world was bigger and better than the one they were exposed to in their daily lives. Dr. Arthur and Michael D'Andre left the program in its second year and I was very fortunate to recruit three superb Ph.D. psychologists: Drs. Lorraine Williams Greene, who became a most effective director of the program, Shiela Peters, and Shelton Smith. The program offered the participants enrichment programs like computer literacy, academic tutoring, job readiness skills, and also enhancements like family life education and workshops in self-esteem and conflict resolution. We hoped that if we improved their skills and raised their self-esteem, the young people might begin to insist on a better future for themselves, to feel entitled, as all children should, to hope. The objectives of the program were formulated in terms of life options and personal and community responsibility.

I tried to think what my kids were seeing and doing and learning when they were ten, eleven, and twelve. What was I doing in Pine Bluff that helped me strive for various productive goals? I remembered the thrill of discovery I had had as a young boy watching the airplanes take off at Tony's field, that sense that the world was infinitely expandable, and I realized that part of the deprivation of being poor is that one's world is terribly constricted, as if there is nothing out there.

As soon as we got the program going, we took our participants on field trips, and the first trip was to the Nashville airport. Such a very simple and easy thing to do, and yet something that the kids had never done. Why would they? How many of these poor young-sters would ever have a reason to go to an airport? They had no money to buy a ticket for themselves and most probably would know few people who travel by plane. They loved seeing the throngs of people bustling about the airport, black people and white people, women and men, many with children, and they sensed the excitement that accompanies traveling. It was an adven-ture for them to see an airplane close up, rather than on TV, and to experience the noise of the takeoff and landing.

They were told to pick out one plane, watch its takeoff, and fol-low its flight into the yonder until the plane was no longer visible. Then I said, "This plane has just flown into the future, a future that could include you as a passenger, or even as the pilot, male or female, one day." Our message was: Look, kids, it's a big world out there and you can be part of it—if you prepare for it, and we will help you prepare.

When the kids came back from the airport and the other places we took them, and told their friends in the housing projects about it, more kids became interested in participating in the program. The Future kids traveled to Disney World, to Washington, D.C., to Atlanta, and these trips became hooks for the other, more serious aspects of what we wanted to do with and for them. Calvin Peters, a counselor in the program, goes with the kids when they take their trips and tells me that the trips give him an opportunity to spend extended time with them, where they can talk to him and share their thoughts. The counselors, really the entire program, function like an extended family, a place for advice and discipline and love, which is just as it should be. It's becoming increasingly clear that programs that enhance self-esteem are most successful when they are long-term, so that there is sufficient time for bonding to occur.

Naturally it's not all fun and field trips. Integral to the program is a tutoring component for schoolwork. My family monitored my schoolwork when I was growing up, and I was taught that I could go out to play only after my work was done. I didn't realize it as a child—how could I?—that such a work ethic is part of a privileged middle-class upbringing. I wanted the I Have a Future kids to have that privilege too.

The program is made attractive to our students through enticements, like the field trips, pizza parties for report card results, auctions, etc., which allow us to reach them with our enhancements, the programs we devise for enrichment. As Calvin explains to them: "If you want to do this, you got to do that."

The adolescents who participate in the program go on to college or some other kind of advanced training, like the military service or to good jobs. In 1995, twenty kids were accepted and enrolled in college from two housing projects that probably had not produced twenty college students even in the last ten years. There were a few senior boys who were unsure about their grades and their status; as soon as Calvin learned about their situation, he, as he would say, put his knuckles on them, and worked with them, and they graduated. We stress education, and post–high school training because that's the key to success in America. I transmit to the kids my father's advice to me: Education is the key to unlocking doors which would otherwise remain closed—be it by race or by poverty. The typical high school dropout rate for the kids in the public housing project is 50 percent by senior year, while the kids involved with I Have a Future seldom drop out.

During the Senate hearings for the Surgeon General nomination, people were confused about the program, or seemed to be. They said the success we'd seen in the group of kids who participated couldn't be viewed as a result of the program. They said it was self-selection, that the kids who'd agreed to be in the program were already the sort of kids who wouldn't drop out. But 100 percent of the kids in our program stayed in school. How could it not count? Certainly some proportion of these very same kids would not have made it without our help. I informed the Senate committee members that even if the response was the result of self-selection, had the I Have a Future program not been in place, there would have been nothing from which to self-select. Because we were there, and because they knew enough to take advantage of our program, these kids have the kinds of futures now that they might otherwise not have had.

It's not just the kids, it's the entire society that's at a disadvantage when a lack of education limits a person's options. The value of offering deprived children an education was reinforced for me a few years ago when I went to a reception in honor of my late friend and flying instructor from Tuskegee, Chief Charles Anderson. It was held at the Smithsonian Air and Space Museum, where Chief, an African-American, was finally being recognized for his work with the Tuskegee Airmen and his contribution to aviation. That evening he was presented with the nation's highest aviation education award, the Brewer Trophy.

The keynote address for the occasion was delivered by Chuck Yaeger, himself a World War II fighter pilot and ace, and the first person to break the sound barrier. Chuck spoke of being poor, of being the son of a coal miner from West Virginia. He told us that he'd thought a lot about how different his life would have been without his excellent public education, that he would never have been able to go to college or make the kind of contribution he did to this country's war effort. I am absolutely convinced that some of our Future kids will make such contributions too.

When, in 1991, we received notification that the I Have a Future program had been awarded one of President Bush's Thousand Points of Light for community service innovations, we were all delighted, the children most of all. The national recognition was wonderful for them. Especially nice for me was that the Secretary of Health and Human Services who came to personally deliver the award to us was Louis Sullivan, a college classmate and good friend. The legacy of Morehouse, Dr. Mays's admonition to dare to dream, seemed very real to us both that day.

Everything was going so well with my work at Meharry—running the department, working on various committees, overseeing my major research grants, guiding the I Have a Future program, and, as always, tending to my patients—that I thought it might be time to rest on my laurels for a bit, but it was not to be. The president of Meharry, David Satcher, called me one morning and asked if he could come and see me in my office. I knew he wanted to ask a favor of me; otherwise I would have been going to him.

Indeed, as soon as he sat down, he said, "Hank, I'm calling in my chips." He reminded me of how I had recruited him to Meharry by persuading him that he was badly needed. He said he wanted me to become special assistant to the president, and then dean of the medical school, because it was becoming more and more essential that there be a merger between Meharry and the city-county hospital. Now I was "badly needed," he said, to help make it happen. Meharry simply didn't have enough patients to train its residents and he knew that if we didn't have access to more patients our various accreditations would be at risk.

His request would involve very big changes in my life. I would have to give up the obstetrical portion of my practice; babies don't wait until a convenient time in between meetings to be born. I would have to give up doing surgery because I would be too involved with administrative duties. I would have to stop teaching; there would be no time for it. I knew I would lose control over my own schedule, and that there would be many other unanticipated sacrifices involved as well.

Trying to forge a merger would be a tremendous project, requiring tremendous amounts of time, and if successful, it would be a tremendous coup for the school. Certainly it was not going to be an easy task either. In fact, my professional friends, when I told them about it, were quick to tell me that we didn't have a snowball's chance in hell of getting the merger accomplished. For me, them's fighting words, and I decided that I had to accept the challenge, especially since David thought that having me be part of the negotiating team would make a difference.

David believed that I could make a contribution because, being on the faculty of Vanderbilt, I was well known to the powers that be there. Since we needed to negotiate with Vanderbilt, David thought that I would be more difficult to disregard than a total stranger. He was calling on me to be a builder of bridges, as a part of the community of North Nashville and Meharry and also as someone connected to the larger and more mainstream medical establishment associated with Vanderbilt.

The background against which the merger negotiation took place was riddled with racism and elitism, making it all the more urgent that the old system be overturned. Meharry and Vanderbilt medical schools had been founded within one year of each other—Vanderbilt in 1875 and Meharry in 1876. Meharry had first attempted to gain access to the city-county hospital in 1893; at that time, the reason given for refusing this request was that the city didn't want blacks staffing their hospital. Back then, people said such things openly.

Consequently, for over a hundred years, Nashville had marginalized and isolated Meharry medical school. Shortly after World War II ended, a Veterans Administration hospital for Nashville was planned. Meharry again asked for access to it, but the city again refused, and erected it on Vanderbilt's campus. Thus, Nashville had two medical colleges, Meharry and Vanderbilt, and, as of 1947, two public hospitals, the Nashville VA hospital and the city-county hospital, the Metropolitan Nashville General Hospital—but only one of the medical schools, Vanderbilt, serviced the two hospitals.

Now the time was right to propose a merger between the two institutions because the city of Nashville had a serious problem. Patients were being treated in a deteriorating facility that would cost the city a fortune to rebuild. The city was paying the city-county hospital for providing health care to the poor, absorbing all the indigent care costs for patients seen in the hospital. Vanderbilt was not eager to give up its exclusive rights to the hospital, partially because the city was giving it $13 or $14 million a year toward faculty salary supplements. This was a great deal to give up, irrespective of its unfairness.

Meharry had a wonderful new facility but didn't have a way to pay for the health care of the many poor people we were treating. As a historically black institution, one that trained primarily black physicians, Meharry attracted patients who were almost exclusively poor and black, and poor and white; yet it was not funded to take care of them.

We thought we had something the city needed, the facility, and the city could provide us with something that we needed, funding for the health care of the poor. When we heard that people were saying that the city had a problem, we realized that somehow "the city" didn't include Meharry. Redefinition was in order. Meharry and the community it serviced were indeed a part of the city, and if "the city" had a problem, we had the solution—merger.

We knew that simply explaining that it was wrong for one school to have sole access to both public hospitals and the other not to have any access at all was futile. We needed some leverage to wrest control from them, and nothing readily presented itself. We couldn't even get the Metropolitan Hospital board to put our requests on the agenda, so we devised a different strategy. We went public.

Our first meeting was with the Rotary Club in 1988, with David Satcher explaining how the merger would benefit *all* the citizens of Nashville. The situation quickly attracted national press coverage, and when the power structure of the city, and of the hospitals, saw Nashville splashed across the front pages of *The New York Times* and *The Washington Post* as a racist city, a change of thinking occurred. The business community, especially, realized that supporting the merger was in the best interests of the city. We were invited to begin a series of meetings to explore the merger possibilities.

The racist aspects involved in preventing the merger were so thinly veiled that I found I could use them to some advantage. In the heat of this confrontation, during a closed negotiating session with Gene Fowinkle, David Satcher, Ike Robinson, the chancellor of Vanderbilt, I said, "Now, Ike, you've really got to support us on this merger because Meharry deserves this."

He remained unconvinced.

I said, "I know that Vanderbilt is trying to do what Duke University has done and that you're trying to emulate them academically and in sports. But, Ike, I can tell you, you're not going to win any national basketball championships without top black players. And if you don't support us on this, I'll have to go public and tell every newspaper and every black kid in the state and beyond not to go to this racist school." I was smiling, but I think he knew I was serious.

The newspaper editorials about the merger were mixed at first, but as the news of the negotiations became more public, the blatant unfairness and wrongness of the anti-merger position became obvious. Although the administrators and board at the hospital were comfortable with their white doctors and didn't want black people telling their staff what to do, it became clear that the board of the city-county hospital needed to negotiate with us whether they liked it or not because public opinion would be too strong against them if they didn't. So the people at the city-county hospital took another tack, one reminiscent of those fairy tales in which people are sent out to do impossible feats before they can win the pot of gold. We were given a list of seemingly impossible conditions that would have to be satisfied before we could think of supplying services to the hospital.

The hospital had very active emergency and ambulatory services and many hospital admissions. In order to take care of such a large number of patients, we were told that we needed to recruit fifty-six new physicians, of whom 80 percent had to be board certified, with the other 20 percent on a board-certification track. That is a daunting number of doctors to have to recruit to a small minority medical college with limited financial resources.

"Okay, no problem," I said. "What else?"

Additionally, we would need eighteen new residents, the only portion of the demands that I didn't think would be too difficult to meet. And we had to have this new faculty in place within just over two years.

We needed funding for these new positions, but that wasn't our biggest problem; it was finding well-qualified doctors who would pick up and move on very short notice. I was the dean of the medical school and thus it was specifically my job to find and place these new physicians, and in a hurry.

The job required all my energy and ingenuity and powers of persuasion. First of all I had to let everyone in the medical community know I was recruiting, and so I placed ads in all the major national medical journals and sent over 1,500 flyers to deans of the 124 other medical schools all over the country. I went to national medical meetings and enlisted the help of the Meharry National Alumni Association to get the word out. Within six months, virtually everyone connected with academic medicine knew what was going on in Nashville at Meharry. I labeled this the "awareness" phase of the recruiting process.

The "engagement" phase was deployed when a prospective faculty member made contact. I made sure that all correspondence and curricula vitae came to me because I was so familiar with what the city and Vanderbilt officials were looking for. After screening an applicant, I would send the application on to the appropriate departmental chair. If anyone inquired about the job, I would send out a detailed letter describing the 116 years of service that Meharry had given the primarily minority community in Nashville, the history of how Vanderbilt had access to the two public hospitals and Meharry didn't, and the outline of our hopes and aspirations for a more equitable and successful future once (if) the merger could be accomplished.

We recognized how difficult it was for most people to uproot their lives, and tried to provide support in whatever way possible. This included helping spouses find employment in the area and supplying our candidates with information about housing, schools, religious institutions, shopping centers, cultural attractions, etc. In short order, we became Nashville's biggest advertisers. All in all, 408 physicians from around the country contacted Meharry about positions, and from this pool we were able to cull and then recruit the fifty-six physicians that were required. Without the help of Audrey Manley and Clay Simpson and others with the Public Health Service, our recruitment task would have been even more difficult.

The doctors who eventually filled the positions were not abandoned after they signed on the dotted line. This was not my way, and I wanted the new staff to know that we would continue to support them through what I called the "placement" phase of moving a life from one locale and community to another. I thought it was not only the nice thing to do but the right thing to do, to maintain the same level of interest in these doctors after they had decided to join the faculty as was maintained during the engagement process.

As thoughtful as I tried to be about reducing anxiety, I was not above applying some heavy pressure on people I knew well. When I found that I needed a new chair for the obstetrics and gynecology department, I contacted Elwyn Grimes. I had shown him his first delivery while he was a Meharry student on rotation in Tuskegee and had been impressed with him immediately. In turn he had evidently been impressed with obstetrics, which had become his specialty. He later went on to Harvard for his postgraduate subspecialty training in reproductive endocrinology, after which I'd recruited him to Meharry in the mid-1970s. After three years with us, he'd left for another position in Kansas City, and now I wanted him back.

I called him in Kansas City and asked, "What are you doing tomorrow? Can we have lunch?" Surprised at the unexpected invitation, he said yes and asked what was going on. "I'll tell you tomorrow," I said, and hung up. The following day, I flew up to see him. "You've made enough money," I told him. "Meharry needs you. You've got to come back and help." And he did.

I was thrilled about the new faculty, and not only because one of the obstacles for the merger was overcome. I was thrilled because Meharry would be enhanced by this new pool of excellent and sophisticated talent; departments would be bolstered, teaching would be more diverse and intense, students would have more opportunities for mentored training, both inpatient and outpatient services would be extended.

Virtually no one expected us to be successful; in fact, I am sure they counted on our failure. But the demands were met, the obstacles overcome, and so the merger had to go through. Meharry has been providing all services to the city-county hospital since 1993, and, to the astonishment of the establishment over there, the sun still rises in the east.

*   *   *

When David Satcher left Meharry to head the CDC, I served as acting president while the search committee sought a replacement for him. Quite a bit of pressure was put on me by members of the board of trustees and others to put my name into the hat for the presidency, and although it was not exactly what I had wanted to do with the next years, I did apply. I felt that I had an obligation to see the merger through, and if there was any way I could do that, I thought I should. But I was not chosen as president.

After the enormous amount of energy I had expended on the merger, I was exhausted. The work had been arduous and time-consuming, but I had worked hard before. I think what caused my exhaustion was the tension of working in an environment where there was so much acrimony. I had been patronized and conde-scended to many times in my life by people who didn't know any better; but with the merger, there were people who were fighting against what was right because of their prejudices and their greed; this was the first time I really was forced to interact with people who were unreasonably committed to our failure.

I decided to take a well-earned sabbatical break, my first in thirty-eight years, and contacted Roger Bulger, someone I knew through my connection with the Institute of Medicine. He invited me to do research at the Association of Academic Health Centers in Washington and I gladly accepted. Working with him, Marian Osterweis, and their staff proved to be one of my most gratifying and rewarding professional enterprises. My research concern was to explore the effect of the gender shift in the physician workforce and to study the implications for health-care reform in this country. In only one generation women admitted to medical school had grown from a mere 7 percent in the 1960s to 49 percent in 1993, a seven-fold increase. It seemed like an important topic to investigate.

It was in Washington, while I was quietly doing research and minding my own business, that I was tapped for the job of Surgeon General, and my education about the pitfalls of the political process began.

PART III

ONE DOOR CLOSES
AND ANOTHER OPENS

CHAPTER SEVEN

Nothing Personal

THE SENATE HEARINGS

In mid-December 1994, I received a call from Philip Lee, the Assistant Secretary for Health in the Department of Health and Human Services, who informed me that there was a search underway for a new Surgeon General. Would I be interested in the position? I had never given the question any thought, I told him, and I would have to talk to my family before making a decision.

Of course, it was flattering to be considered for such a post—there are over 400,000 doctors in this country—but I have read a great deal of political science and history. Politics, I knew, was a predatory and sometimes ugly business; I had just been through the merger process and I didn't know if I could tolerate more dissension in my life. Sandy didn't think it was a good idea; being out front in the limelight never appealed to her at all, but I had always believed that one of the responsibilities of living in a democracy is participating in the political process. For me, that meant if the President of the United States calls on you, you answer that call. I had taught my children, and sincerely believe, that one can't complain about government unless one is willing to get in there and do something to change things. If good people don't participate, things will only get worse.

I told Secretary Lee that I would be honored to be considered. There were forms to fill out, my fingerprints were taken, and my tax returns were examined. I was asked some general questions, versions of "Is there anything in your background that could embarrass the President?" I didn't think I had any unseemly ghosts in my closets, certainly nothing earthshaking; but I suspect neither Lani Guinier nor Zoë Baird would have anticipated the brouhaha that accompanied their nominations either, so it was somewhat difficult to be completely sure. After this initial spate of activity, nothing more happened and I promptly forgot all about it. Many candidates were being considered, and I thought the process of settling on a particular nominee would take a great deal of time.

On January 29, I was visiting my dear friend Warren Pearse, who had recently retired as executive director of the American College of Obstetricians and Gynecologists. I was spending the day with him and his wife, Mary, visiting the Naval Academy at Annapolis, looking at the beautiful chapel there and then lunching at a restaurant with a view of Chesapeake Bay. As is my habit when I have been out of contact for a few hours, I called my office to check in. My secretary, Cynthia Spriggs, answered the phone and most uncharacteristically and quite shrilly demanded to know where I was. "Visiting Annapolis," I told her.

"Get back here," she said, "right away." It was obvious that something had happened, and I asked her what was the matter. "The President wants to see you."

"What president?" I asked, which in retrospect seems idiotic but at the time was perfectly sensible, as it could have been any number of presidents of various organizations and societies and the furthest thing from my mind was that the President of the United States was calling me.

Cynthia was having none of this. She said, "You know perfectly well what President. He wants to know if he can see you at five o'clock today." This time, I got it.

I rejoined my friends and told them that the President wanted to see me, quickly got back to my Washington apartment to make myself presentable, and drove to the White House. Wherever I go, I bring a book to read, because I have learned from experience to use idle moments profitably; if I don't, there simply won't be enough hours in the day to accomplish everything I want to accomplish. This occasion was no exception.

As excited as I was to be sitting in the White House waiting for the President, I became so engrossed in my book, *Sleepwalking Through History,* by Haynes Johnson, that I didn't realize that someone had entered the room. When I looked up, President Clinton was smiling and greeting me. He asked me what I was reading, and when I told him, he said that he had read it also and was curious about my reaction to the book. I responded that I hadn't really learned anything new, that the book simply reaffirmed opinions I'd already had. President Clinton said he felt much the same way. We were off to a good start.

The President was familiar with the basic facts of my life, that I was from Arkansas and that I had been inducted at an early age into the Institute of Medicine, etc., but he didn't know my specific views on a number of health issues and so he inquired about them. We spoke about teen pregnancy, and I told him that I believed the epidemic in our country was the result of socioeconomic and political issues, not purely medical ones, and that we had to overcome certain attitudes that actually prevented patients from receiving the best possible health care before we could make any serious progress. I had some concrete suggestions about how to accomplish this, which we discussed.

I told him we needed a national campaign designed to reduce teen pregnancy, and a government commitment to support grassroots interventions; Washington would play a central role by allocating Federal resources and expertise to assist individual communities in finding ways to prevent teen pregnancy. Nashville's I Have a Future program could serve as a model for other communities as well.

Our meeting was most congenial, and after more conversation the President asked me if I would like a personal tour of the White House. We discussed the renovations to the White House, which I was somewhat familiar with because I had read David McCullough's biography of Harry Truman, the President who had over-seen many of the improvements. On some level I realized that what seemed like a casual conversation was, in essence, an interview, and I knew that if our collaboration was going to be successful, I had to interview him too. I noted with some relief that President Clinton was enormously likable, personable, witty, and smart, and I was confident that we would be able to work well together.

Our talk covered a broad range of subjects, including, for example, our mutual admiration for Winston Churchill. He seemed especially intrigued by my admiration for Churchill's capacity for catching complex thoughts in a perfect phrase. Like what? I related one of my favorite quotes. During World War II, after England had been bombed almost continuously for a year, and still the Germans had been unable to break this tough island nation, the bombing finally slowed. The bulldog of the British Isles went to the airwaves and said, "My fellow Britons. This is not the end. This is not even the beginning of the end. But, ah, it is the end of the beginning." Churchill had found a way to quantify an intangible.

Although I was enjoying our discussion, I began to think I was taking up an inappropriate amount of the President's time. He was a busy man, and certainly had better things to do, I thought, than to chat with me about books and quotations; but each time I got up and excused myself, the President told me to relax and we talked some more. I imagine he liked what he heard, because after about an hour or so, he put his hand on my shoulder and said with some formality that he wanted to nominate me for the position of Surgeon General of the United States. With a formality matching his, I told him I accepted the nomination.

As I prepared to leave, he brought me two beautiful green leather-bound books on the history of the White House, and told me that since I had expressed an interest in the subject, he thought I might like them. When I asked him when I had to return them, he said, very simply, "You don't. They are a gift." It was a thoughtful and personal gesture that touched me.

On the day of the official announcement, February 2, 1995, the

President, Secretary of Health and Human Services, Donna Shalala, and I held a brief press conference, at which I was introduced to the level of ready repartee that one needs to master in order to communicate with and through the media. Almost immediately, the President was asked whether he had told me not to discuss certain issues in public. The way the question was put was something like "In view of the problems you have had with your former Surgeon General, Dr. Joycelyn Elders, have you instructed Dr. Foster to be circumspect in his responses?"

The President hesitated just for a moment. In fact, he had never come right out and explicitly articulated that he hoped I would be more politically attuned than my good friend Joycelyn. Nevertheless, I knew quite well that he expected me to behave with greater political astuteness. As a kind of joke, I leaned over to the microphone while the President was still thinking and said, "No comment." Everyone laughed, and the President smiled and said, "I can't do any better than that."

If my initial encounter with the media was a success, it certainly didn't last long. The week following the announcement was a nightmare. All the reading of political history in the world could not have prepared me for the subsequent intense political scrutiny that I had to undergo, or for the viciousness of the attacks on my character and my life. It was really quite maddening to me that anyone could get up and say something terrible about me, in the press or elsewhere, and that I would be forced to respond to the accusation, no matter how nonsensical it was.

Senator Joseph Biden of Delaware, for example, one of my early attackers, didn't know a damn thing about me. In fact, I could have waltzed in and danced on his chest and he wouldn't have known who I was; yet he managed to have a lot of negative opinions about my nomination. His position was so inappropriately precipitous that he ended up having to recant his initial statement, saying he would have to withhold judgment until he learned some facts. Good idea, I thought, but a little late.

I remember remonstrating with Mike Berman, one of the people hired by the White House to help me prepare for the hearing process, complaining that "anybody can get up and say that I stole a car three years ago in Toledo, and now I've got to go out and prove that I didn't, that I've never even been in Toledo. How can that be?"

Mike's response was surprising, and very useful to me. He smiled broadly and said very slowly, "Because this is a democracy."

I realized that he was right and vowed to deal with the accusations with as much grace as I could muster. But it wasn't easy, and my wife suffered terribly during the process. How could she not? I was being attacked unfairly, by perfect strangers, and she took it personally and was upset. I wasn't as distressed; I knew that the attacks were driven by politics and weren't really about me.

It was absolutely clear that I was about to be a proxy in an abortion debate and in the upcoming 1996 presidential race. Ralph Reed, the executive director of the Christian Coalition, declared my nomination "dead" almost immediately. The Republican presidential hopefuls, led by Senators Bob Dole and Phil Gramm, hoping to display to the anti-choice people how tough they were, jumped right on board with Reed, declaring their opposition.

On the other side, leaders of pro-choice movements like Planned Parenthood and the National Abortion Rights and Reproductive Action League, as well as women's groups all over the country, applauded my credentials, saying it was about time a candidate was put forward who was concerned with women's health issues. These groups were adamant that doctors specializing in obstetrics/gynecology should not be precluded from entering public service because constitutionally protected procedures, like abortions, might have been part of their professional responsibilities.

I was inexperienced about the process—as Senator Christopher Dodd of Connecticut put it, not "media wise"—and I had to learn quickly, on my feet. Unfortunately, one of my first steps caused me to trip and start an avalanche, and although I did everything in my power to regain my footing, I lost a tremendous amount of ground. What happened was that quite innocently I made a throwaway remark to the public relations people of the Department of Health and Human Services as we were casually sitting around drinking coffee. Someone asked me if I had ever done any abortions. I laughed and said, "Yeah. I'm an obstetrician/gynecologist." These people had my résumé; I assumed that they had read it.

I actually thought that the question arose from curiosity about abortions, and medical educator that I am, I proceeded to recount a story of one of the incidents I remembered best. The reason that this particular case was memorable to me was that I thought it illustrative of the dynamic nature of medical knowledge and practice, and how, as doctors, we need to be constantly educating ourselves.

A young woman with a master's degree had been diagnosed with AIDS and came to me requesting that her early pregnancy be terminated. At that time it was believed that pregnancy accelerated the rate of progression of the AIDS process, and this poor woman wanted to stay alive as long as she could. Since abortions were the accepted intervention in such cases, and since in America it's a woman's private decision how she chooses to respond to such matters, the abortion was accomplished. I thought the story interesting.

Lo and behold, somebody who was at that meeting went directly to the press and announced that Dr. Foster said that he has only done one abortion in his entire career! I couldn't believe it. Was it really possible that none of the men who were serving as advisors realized that most ob/gyn doctors perform abortions? Who did they think were doing them?

The media were more astute and asked if the number—one—was really accurate. "No," I said. The PR people then wanted to know how many abortions I had done. I had no idea, and I told them exactly that: "I don't know." There was some urgency to come up with a number, they said, because a right-to-life group had circulated a memo all over Capitol Hill which said that I had done over seven hundred abortions. "Was that true?"

"Of course not," I answered.

They asked me to guess. I was new to all this, and I usually try to be accommodating. Since the staff people who were responsible for helping me asked me to guess, I guessed. Big mistake, as it turned out. What is obvious to me now should have been perfectly obvious to them then—I should never have been asked to guess.

"Over a hundred?" someone inquired.

"No, not that many," I said helpfully.

"Well," they pushed, "a dozen?"

"Yeah," I said, "maybe a dozen." The exact number couldn't be critical, I thought, since everything I had done was perfectly legal and fully documented. I assumed that they must have been asking for a general rather than a specific number.

The next thing I knew, Health and Human Services had written a document, over my signature, that stated that I had done exactly twelve abortions.

The fiasco that erupted was really the result of stupidity. There was no reason on earth to guess about something that would turn out to be so controversial. Every procedure I had ever performed was recorded and written down. All one had to do was count.

I can slip up once or twice, but not three times. It quickly became evident that guessing was disastrous, and I realized that I had better not rely on anyone other than myself. And Sandy. Together with Meharry's record librarian we went through all of the records and found that I had been listed as "physician of record" on thirty-nine abortion cases. In a teaching hospital, it is typical for a resident to do such procedures, and indeed in twenty-nine of those recorded cases, there was a resident involved in the case. My memory was, in fact, not so cloudy; with my own hands, I had probably done fewer than a dozen over the entire thirty-eight-year period.

With newspapers throughout the country running sensational stories about my inability to recall the number of abortions I had performed, I went on *Nightline* to speak directly to the people—"in my own defense," as Ted Koppel headlined the program. The show was taped in the Roosevelt Room of the White House to reinforce the Administration's allegiance to and support of my candidacy.

Koppel pointed out that it "probably should have occurred" to someone in the Administration that I had performed abortions and that the way the abortion issue had been handled, or rather, as he put it, "botched," had offered my opponents, and the President's, a basis on which to reject the nomination. I told Ted Koppel that I had made an honest mistake in initially guessing rather than checking the records and that I certainly never had any intention of trying to deceive anyone. I sincerely apologized for my naiveté and informed him and the public that I had researched the records and that the official number of abortions that I was responsible for was thirty-nine.

I also said what was most important: that I abhorred abortion, and that I had spent my entire professional life trying to deliver healthy babies who were loved and wanted by their parents. He asked me about condom distribution, and I told him that I believed in abstinence first, that abstinence was the very foundation of the I Have a Future program. In the very short amount of time allotted to me, eleven minutes in all, I tried to do what I could to counteract the spate of negative media attention I had received in the previous five days. I proclaimed that more than anything else I believed in the teaching of values and that, along with President Clinton, I thought that abortions should be safe, legal, and rare. I had had firsthand experience with what illegal and unsafe abortions did to the poor women who were savaged by them, and I never wanted to see that again.

But politics is relentlessly unforgiving. The numbers blunder became an excuse for my opponents to open fire, and the only artillery I had available to me was my record of integrity and service. The accusations against me must have made for good media coverage, because there were numerous articles about what a monster I was: how I had sterilized unsuspecting women, and performed zillions of abortions, that I was an advocate of randomly distributing contraceptives to children, that Meharry's I Have a Future program had actually increased sexual activity and the incidence of pregnancy—all kinds of idiocy. The most offensive and really outrageous accusation made against me was that I had participated in a cover-up of the infamous Tuskegee syphilis study.

Right-wing zealots spent a great deal of time and energy making sure the public was blitzed with inaccurate information about me, and I had to find a way to defend myself against these unwarranted attacks. I thought that the intense indignation of the people bent on maligning me seemed a bit hollow; their concern somewhat spurious. Where was their outrage about the extraordinary number of poor black babies who had died from lack of health care in the rural areas of this country, like Tuskegee? Where were they when I was working to do something about this? To my mind, these people were spouting rhetoric for political purposes and I didn't really think they gave a damn about either the women or the children I had worked a lifetime to help. My nomination was being used to support the political agenda of those opposed to abortion.

Although many positive articles were written about my background and accomplishments, these did not have nearly as much of an impact as the negative ones. I was most eager to tell my side of the story and used the weeks before the scheduled Senate committee hearings to speak personally to as many members of Congress as I could.

Standard in any nomination process are "Hill visits," where the candidate meets personally with members of Congress to answer any lingering questions they might have. I like to think that I am a pretty good communicator and now I wanted to use these skills to change my image in the press. So I used these visits to attempt to redress the so-called credibility gap that the media and the anti-choice lobby were promulgating around my nomination. The White House advisors who were helping me prepare warned me that these visits could be quite unpleasant—"icy cold"—but that didn't matter to me. I hoped once the senators met me, once we had the chance to converse, it wouldn't be quite so easy to treat me as a political football.

Senators, like many people, can be wedded to their opinions and prejudices, and I was not always welcomed with open arms. One memorable meeting was with a Republican senator who was opposed to my nomination. The day we spoke I happened to be wearing a pink-ribbon lapel pin and the conservative senator pointed to it and explained to me that what was wrong with this country was that there was no morality, "all this AIDS business."

I was polite. I said, "Senator, this is an emblem for the fight against breast cancer. It has nothing to do with AIDS."

I told him that the AIDS-fighting symbol was larger and red.

His reply was a harangue about how morality was breaking down in this country and "those people got what they deserved."

I was still polite, but it was getting harder to maintain my composure. I said, "Senator, do you know that almost a quarter of the people in this country with AIDS are children. Certainly you don't think they are responsible also, do you?" He didn't have a ready response.

I was appalled. How could a person with such limited views be an elected official? This is the result, I thought to myself, of the fact that only one out of three Americans consistently votes. And so archconservatives, who get out the vote more than other groups, have far more relative influence in policy positions than is representative of the majority view.

My meeting with Senator Nancy Kassebaum, who would be chairing the Committee on Labor and Human Resources, the Senate committee charged with evaluating my nomination, was disturbing in a different way. She is a pro-choice Republican, and was Bob Dole's junior colleague from Kansas; I'm sure she had conflicting loyalties. If she followed the Republican party line, she would vote against me, supporting Senator Dole's stand against my nomination. However, since she was pro-choice, it would be difficult for her to quash my nomination just because I supported the hard-won policy of reproductive choice for women.

Senator Kassebaum described how grueling and upsetting the nomination process could be, how my background would be minutely dissected, and how horrendously long and drawn-out every inquiry would be. I was not dissuaded and reassured her that my background check would be fine.

Given the problem I represented to her, I think she would have been happy if I'd simply disappeared, and it was my impression that she was tacitly encouraging me to withdraw my nomination. While I understood clearly that doing so would certainly make her life easier, as well as the lives of most Republicans, somehow I did not find this a terribly compelling reason to withdraw.

In fact I had no intention of withdrawing. As every ob/gyn knows, withdrawal is rarely an effective method of doing anything. Furthermore, I thought withdrawal cowardly. It was not even a temptation. I was certainly not going to slink away from a hard fight when I had the Future kids watching me and supporting me. Politics may be dirty and difficult and complicated and hurtful and unfair, but even so, people have to participate or the system just won't work. I was staying. Even if the system didn't work for me personally, I wasn't about to abandon it. I wanted the Future kids to see that I really practiced what I preached.

Even in the midst of all this I realized that the system works more often than not, even if things don't always come out in your favor. One of my favorite quotes from Winston Churchill is most apt. He used to complain terribly about the democratic system. He said that democracy is really the worst system ever devised— except for all the others. I agreed wholeheartedly.

My Hill visits were not all difficult; in fact I discovered that I had many friends. Democratic women were my staunchest supporters: Patty Murray, Barbara Mikulski, Barbara Boxer, Carol Moseley-Braun, and Dianne Feinstein, among others, spoke out in favor of my nomination and tried to pressure Senator Dole to allow me a full Senate vote, which he had threatened to deprive me of. A member of the administrative staff told me that some of the congress-women had given me a wonderful compliment, saying that they felt that I could have been their doctor, delivering their babies and supervising their health care. People didn't always look at every nominee in such personal terms, I was told. It's rare to meet a candidate recommended for, let's say, Defense Secretary, and think, hey, I want that man to defend me.

Not all my friends were female, by any means. I was very pleased with my visit to Democratic Senator Howell Heflin of Alabama, who was a supporter of my nomination. I wanted to see him because I had lived in Alabama during an important part of my medical life, and I wished to shake his hand.

What struck me most about his office was his staff, not only their competence and graciousness but also their racial diversity. There were many African-Americans and I could sense that these people were not brought in because it was good politics to do so. Senator Heflin seemed to have a genuine appreciation for the skills and work ability of the members of his staff—quite a turnaround from the Alabama I had known in 1965.

Senator Edward Kennedy and his staff were also most impressive and admirable. Everyone seemed bright and interested in learning the truth about me; that was refreshing. I liked the senator from Massachusetts enormously; there was nothing phony or fake about him. He was supporting my nomination because he had read about my life and was impressed with what I had tried to accomplish during my career. He said that he sensed I was a decent and honest person who had done nothing in my life, intentionally, that would have hurt anyone, and he thought I was getting very bad treatment from the media. I was most appreciative of his support and compassion.

Indeed many senators did not approve of the way I had been treated, and their support was extraordinary. The only responsibility Democrats had in order to honor their commitment to their party and to the President was to cast a vote for me—if they ever had the opportunity. They certainly didn't have to go out and fight with their colleagues on my behalf, the way Senator J. James Exon of Nebraska, for example, did. He went onto the Senate floor and excoriated his colleagues: if they allowed my nomination to die an unseen death, it would be an ignoble way to behave. He said that I deserved better, that I was a good person and I deserved my vote before the full Senate. The White House staff people were surprised at the level of support I received on the Hill, which, considering the outcome of the process, was most gratifying.

While all these preparations for the hearings were taking place, I had an unfortunate experience with a few members of the FBI which really frightened me, and it became apparent to me how unprotected the average citizen is against members of a powerful government bureaucracy. Dean Phelus, the manager of the apartment where I was living in Washington, called one day and said that two FBI agents were requesting entry to my apartment. Dean suspected that since I hadn't mentioned this to him, I was unaware of it.

Indeed I was, and grateful for his intelligence, I told him that under no circumstance did the agents have permission to enter my apartment when I wasn't present. The FBI men had told Dean that I had said it was all right. It was definitely not "all right" to attempt to enter my apartment without my knowledge or authorization and, in addition, to attempt to pressure the building manager. I was upset by this callous disregard for my privacy, not because I had anything to hide; I didn't. People had been making inquiries about me and my family for months, but this kind of underhanded sneakiness was unacceptable. I might have been nominated for public office, but that did not mean I had to relinquish my right to privacy.

Donna Shalala and the Department of Health and Human Services investigated my complaint and were told that there had been a misunderstanding. Naturally. According to the FBI, they'd simply been asking whether the manager had the ability to enter the apartment. I may be new to the game, but I am not entirely stupid, and I thought that was the dumbest response I had ever heard. Could a building manager gain entry into one of the apartments in his building? The response was absurd.

Perhaps I was especially uncomfortable and suspicious because I had recently finished reading *The Man and His Secrets,* about J. Edgar Hoover. The agents' arrogance in thinking they were invincible might have been a legacy from the bad old days. I certainly had no idea who these individuals were, or if they were working with or without orders, but I was pretty certain that they were not my friends. It was even possible that these government agents had ideas of their own about me. Maybe they wanted to corrupt the process, or enhance their own careers. Whatever their rationale, I became extremely protective of my family and my personal life.

My repugnance for the very people who were charged with the protection of the people of this country became important when my son Wendell happened upon a threat against my life on the Internet. Someone had entered a remark on one of the bulletin boards which stated that the President was jeopardizing the life of any obstetrician/gynecologist nominated for Surgeon General. Nothing personal against me, the writer said. But since I was the only ob/gyn nominated, I took it quite personally indeed. So did the Administration, who wanted to supply me with protection. Anything but the FBI, I told them; so U.S. marshals shadowed me for three months.

Fighting the unwarranted accusations against me took up most of our time, and the more important issues, what we wanted the people of America to know about my commitment to women, children, adolescents, and other underrepresented groups got drowned out by other noise. When, for example, the First Lady and I initiated a National Immunization Program by together visiting Mary's Center, a Washington, D.C., community clinic which serves primarily the local Hispanic community, we hoped the media would be there; but this event was completely obliterated by coverage of the Oklahoma City bombing, which occurred on the same day. When former Meharry students and alumni came to Washington to visit members of Congress and speak on my behalf, the attention of the press was still diverted.

Some of the I Have a Future kids raised funds to travel by bus to Washington in order to meet with President Clinton, but the O. J. Simpson trial got more attention from the media than their visit. The students were heartbreakingly eloquent when they spoke about what their lives would have been like without the program. They said that they would not be going to college, or having careers, or staying free of drugs, or practicing abstinence if not for our support.

There were tears in the President's eyes when he told these inner-city kids—whom few had ever given a damn about for most of their lives—that he had entertained kings, queens, and prime ministers in the room in which we were standing, but he had never been more proud to have anyone there than he was to have them that day. It was a memorable meeting, but because the media didn't cover the story, few outside the White House heard about it.

These media events were planned, in part, to show the Congress that the White House was committed to my nomination and would stand behind it, even if the road got bumpy. White House support was critical because many Democrats were upset with the way the Administration had backed away from previous nominations, like those of Zoë Baird and Lani Guinier. Democrats might have been reluctant to support a candidate, especially one like me who was unpopular with some of their constituents, if, at the end of the day, the nomination would be moot. Why should they stick their necks out if the President was not going to? It was important that people see that the Administration would not abandon me.

Finally, in May, after months of controversy and delay, the Senate hearings were scheduled to begin. People inquired about whether the prospect of the hearings was giving me butterflies. I answered that what would really have given me butterflies was not to have the hearings. It would have killed me not to have had the opportunity to confront my accusers and reassure my supporters. Lani Guinier, for example, never had that opportunity. I couldn't wait to have mine.

My official introduction to the committee exposed the polarization my nomination had caused. I was unacceptable to some people because I espoused a pro-choice position on abortion, and for others I was the very best candidate for the job because I was a champion of women's rights. The phrase "pawn in the abortion debate" was repeated over and over during the hearings.

Tennessee representative Bob Clement was one of the members of Congress to formally introduce me, and he spoke in favor of my nomination, telling the committee that the Nashville community considered me the quintessential "people's doctor," and he lauded my capacity to be a consensus builder. Clement talked about my commitment to health issues locally and nationally. I had been chairman of a subcommittee on infant mortality as part of the Governor Lamar Alexander's Task Force on Infant Mortality, involved with Partnership 2000, as well as a member of the Ethics Advisory Board for HEW Secretary Joseph Califano. Washington State's Democratic senator, Patty Murray, another of the people who introduced me, said that the country needed a Surgeon General who knew something about the health-care problems of women and children and said that I was a physician with a vision.

But by now I knew enough not to start preening, and indeed the very next person to speak to the committee was Representative Tom Coburn, a Republican from Oklahoma, who claimed that he had nothing against me personally (a familiar refrain) but felt strongly that anyone who condoned abortion or even contraceptive education should not be considered for the Surgeon General's position. Constitution be damned, I suppose. Abortion was immoral, he believed, premarital sex was immoral, and what the country needed was a more moral candidate.

These hearings before the members of the Senate Labor and Human Resources Committee afforded me an opportunity to publicly respond to the accusations that had been brought against me in the media, and I was most eager to present myself. At the outset, I apologized for the confusion concerning the number of abortion procedures I had performed, and I repeated that I had relied on my memory rather than on documentation, and said, again, that I had never had any intention to deceive. There would have been no point to a deception, I reminded the committee, since everything I had done was perfectly legal, aboveboard, and easily verifiable. I had simply made an honest mistake, for which I was sorry.

I took on each of the serious accusations that had been leveled against me. Anti-choice people had tried to make Meharry into some kind of abortion factory, with me as the foreman, because we had participated in a research study for the Upjohn drug company. I explained to the committee that medical colleges frequently are sites for the research and development of new drugs, which is as it should be. Carefully controlled FDA-approved clinical trials supported by physicians and academic medical institutions offer the most responsible methods for evaluating how patients react to untried medications. Meharry Medical College was one of several sites which trialed a new class of medications called prostaglandins.

The point of this particular study was to ensure the safety, efficacy, and patient acceptance of the medication under evaluation. As I had repeated dozens of times before the committee hearings, I believed that abortions should be safe, legal, and rare. The drug being researched would have offered women a safe, noninvasive alternative to surgical abortion, the only option women have at present. I didn't think there was anything to apologize for in supporting such an effort.

The results of the study were reported in a paper which was accepted by a highly prestigious professional journal, the *Journal of Obstetrics and Gynecology,* what we call the Green Journal, after undergoing a rigorous peer review process. Doctors learn from each other through this kind of writing; and having a paper published about the research indicated that there were valuable and important implications from our study.

Accusations were aimed at my other writings too. Another article that I had published, which appeared in the *Southern Medical Journal,* had been unearthed—and misread—by members of the anti-choice lobby. This paper reviewed 485 hysterectomy procedures with the goal of offering guidelines which would reduce the injudicious use of hysterectomy. Avoiding unnecessary surgery was a subject I had been passionate about since medical school, when I had been lucky enough to rescue my mother from having an unnecessary procedure. My position on this subject had remained consistent throughout the years.

Now, however, I had to defend myself. Somehow those opposed to my nomination missed the point of the article, although the very first sentence reads: "Obstetricians and gynecologists must guard vigilantly against the injudicious and indiscriminate removal of the normal uterus." From this academic review they extracted only the fact that four of those instances of hysterectomy had been performed on mentally handicapped women. The cry arose: Foster sterilizes the mentally retarded.

Providing hysterectomies to seriously mentally retarded women who were too handicapped to take good care of themselves was the standard of proper medical care during the 1970s, especially when the doctor had reason to believe that a woman's incapacities were endangering her health. I recounted for the committee one of the cases that I remembered quite well. A very handicapped young woman had been brought to me by her concerned parents because the hygienic problems associated with her menses were causing ulcers to form on her thighs and buttocks. She was suffering from osteomyelitis, an inflammation of the bone and its sheath, which, if untreated, could become fatal. Her parents were justifiably alarmed and requested my help. What should I have done, I asked the committee, sent her home without treatment? The job of doctoring was to offer appropriate help, which is exactly what I did.

The committee had received incorrect information about these cases, and they questioned me on the issue of informed consent, a concept which was developed after these procedures—in fact, partly because of review articles like the one I had written. When people are mentally handicapped, their parents supply consent; this was what occurred with these procedures. They not only provided consent; they begged me for help. I'd call that informed. A prominent bioethicist, Arthur Caplan, offered testimony that I had not only performed my duties properly, according to the standard of care of the day, but further, he said, my approach to the problem was actually enlightened for that era.

By far, the most offensive part of the entire process was the accusation that I had known about the horrendous experiments carried out by Public Health Service researchers in Tuskegee in which poor black men infected with syphilis had been left medically untreated, for experimental purposes, from the 1930s to the 1970s, and that I had participated in some kind of cover-up.

It seems that Dr. McRae, the same doctor who had left Tuskegee following the successful court action I took against him when he wanted to build a new hospital with Hill-Burton funding in order to accommodate his white patients, had told the committee that I had been at a 1969 meeting of the Macon County Medical Society when Public Health Service officials had informed the group about the study. Remarkably, he remembered exactly where I had been sitting, etc.

I certainly didn't recall attending this particular meeting, but thirty years is a long time. I was quite sure about something else, however. Although it was possible that I might have forgotten a routine medical meeting, it was not at all possible that I would have forgotten hearing about a corrupt and offensive trick played by the government on poor black men. Nor would any of the other physicians who'd attended the meeting. Had I known therapy was being withheld from people who needed it, I would have been the first one up in arms. Remember, Tuskegee University (formerly Institute) houses the records of all racial lynchings in this country, and, as a group, we certainly took institutionalized racism quite seriously. In fact, as soon as I learned of the study, in 1972, I took immediate action and mobilized the internists and other doctors in the area to locate and contact the men involved and bring them into treatment.

But no matter how many times I repeated the truth, I had trouble being heard. Senator Dan Coats of Indiana, in particular, either didn't understand what I was saying or was tremendously invested in not believing me. As *The Washington Post* put it, he sat looking down at me with a "hangman's glower" throughout the proceedings. Since Coats had asked President Clinton to withdraw my nomination before the hearings had even started, I was not entirely convinced of his impartiality.

I told the committee the details of how I had actually learned about the Tuskegee experiment. In 1972, as president of the Macon County Medical Society, I was in Montgomery meeting with Dr. Ira Meyers, the director of the Alabama Health Department. We were asked to leave the meeting and speak to the press about a breaking

story of medical importance. Dr. Meyers and I met with the jour-
nalists, who reported the facts of the situation that the Centers for
Disease Control had kept secret for over forty years. What was our
opinion? It was at that time that I first learned of this atrocity.

Now it was my word against Dr. McRae's, and it seemed that for
Senator Coats my word was not good enough. The fact that a class-
action suit had absolved the Macon County Medical Society of any
culpability wasn't either. I was guilty until I could prove myself
innocent. How could I prove that I'd never heard something at a
meeting I couldn't remember? This time, I wasn't about to rely on
memory alone, especially if there was a chance that I could find
documentation.

I came up with what I considered an absolutely brilliant idea and
told the consultants who were part of my nomination support team
to contact the Alabama Bureau of Vital Statistics and get records of
the babies who were delivered on the day of the meeting. The times
of their birth would be recorded on the birth certificates, and therefore so would my presence.

I was able to document from these birth records that I was performing a cesarean section during the time the 1969 meeting was
being held. My patient, Minnie Jameison, sent the committee a
sworn affidavit that I was with her the entire time, which medical
records verified, although Senator Coats seemed to suggest that I
could have traveled, like some energetic James Bond character, in
and out of the medical meeting while simultaneously performing
major surgery on my patient. The incredibly stupid thing about the
entire discussion was that even those doctors who attended the
1969 meeting, including Dr. McRae himself, with his gift of extraordinary memory, had no recollection of anything being said about
withholding treatment from anyone.

The Tuskegee syphilis study was a travesty perpetrated by the
federal government on poor black men (one can be sure that this
population was thought to be more appropriate for this kind of
experimentation than another population—say, a middle-class
white group), and now the government was attempting to blame

the cover-up on the entire medical community, headed by me. We doctors were devoting our lives to making the world a little healthier and safer for this very community, begging the government for monetary support and other resources. No doctor in Tuskegee would have tolerated such a deplorable experiment; in fact, I am sure every doctor would have gone ballistic. I couldn't understand how anyone would have thought we would have turned our backs on the very community we had come to serve.

Even now, after so much time has elapsed since the hearings, it is difficult for me to suppress my outrage at this attack. It was most important to me to conduct myself with dignity throughout the hearings, even when it got ugly. I knew my Future kids were back home watching the process, which made it doubly important that I conduct myself with intelligence and speak with integrity. But I confess that when Dan Coats started hammering at me about the Tuskegee study, I finally lost my cool.

He was spouting all kinds of nonsense, and then asked me, "Am I wrong about that?" At the very end of my patience, I said loudly, "Wrong, sir! Under oath. Wrong. Incorrect. Wrong! Wrong! Wrong!" I guess I thought if I repeated myself enough times he would hear me. This was an attack on my character, about what kind of person I was. In my entire life, this was the first time my sense of morality had ever been impugned.

With all the controversy, the Senate Committee on Labor and Human Resources finally voted to give my nomination a positive recommendation. All seven Democrats voted in my favor, which had been anticipated, but surprisingly two Republicans, Bill Frist and Jim Jeffords, did also, so the final count was nine in favor, seven opposed. Coming out of the committee with a positive recommendation is not enough, as it turns out, to secure a full Senate vote. The nomination process is extremely complex and I certainly don't imagine I understand all the subtleties involved, but as the experts explained to me, it all comes down to the numbers.

According to Senate rules, the Majority Leader is able to decide which piece of legislative business comes up for a vote and when it gets voted on. Senator Dole had said that he would not bring my nomination up for a full Senate debate and vote. Interestingly, now that the hearings were over, and the committee had decided on a favorable recommendation, Dole changed his position about meeting with me and suddenly had some time to do so. My suspicion is that he saw that public opinion was turning in my favor, and he realized that it would be politically unwise for him to kill my nomination without even meeting with me. We had a perfunctory meeting during which he told me, courteously, that he thought I was a good man, but that politics was complicated and hard to understand. I thanked him for seeing me.

Dole was under pressure by many members of Congress to change his mind about preventing my nomination from being voted on. Even those who might not have voted for my confirmation as Surgeon General still thought Dole's position was unpardonable, or, as Senator Dodd said, "childish and stupid" and unfair. Regardless of their stance on abortion, many believed that I should have my day on the Senate floor. The Black Caucus, the Urban Caucus, and the Women's Caucus, especially, put pressure on Dole, but he remained unmoved. Even Nancy Kassebaum, who voted against a positive recommendation for me in committee, thought that I should have a chance at a full Senate vote. Dole went on CBS-TV's *Face the Nation* and said that the position of Surgeon General "isn't important anyway," so I wondered why he had taken so much trouble to block the confirmation process.

My legislative advisors explained that my future depended on the decision of only four or five senators. Hand-to-hand combat, the staffers called it. In order to be confirmed as Surgeon General, I would need fifty-one votes, which, according to party leaders, I had. But because Senator Phil Gramm had promised to filibuster, sixty senators were required to override it, nine more votes than needed for confirmation. The Senate had forty-five Democrats, who would probably vote in favor of my nomination coming up for a full and fair vote. The integrity of the Senate was at stake, some senators felt.

There are many reasons that politicians vote one way or another, and I knew in my case some of them had nothing to do with me or the Surgeon General position. Senators deal favors for each other, a kind of you stay with me on this problem and I will support you on something that is important to you, a political one-hand-washes-the-other maneuver. It would certainly be prudent for many Republicans to stay with Majority Leader Dole. Other senators might have been happy to use the occasion of my nomination to flex their muscles at the White House and show President Clinton that they could sabotage any nomination he made. The anti-abortion lobby wanted my head on a platter and perhaps some senators didn't want to anger that powerful constituency. It didn't help that Douglas Johnson, legislative director of the National Right to Life Committee, threatened that his group would hold senators politically accountable if they voted to stop the filibuster.

Each senator had a unique and distinct agenda, and my confirmation vote was used as a way to deploy whatever strategy seemed most useful to them at that moment. When the final vote was taken, fifty-seven senators voted to stop the filibuster and take the vote, but this number was three short of what was needed. The bottom line is, sometimes you have the votes, and sometimes you don't. I didn't. In the end, my confirmation vote was tabled, and I suppose it remains buried in the docket to this day.

I was terrifically disappointed not to have a chance to have my nomination voted on. Clarence Thomas, whose nomination generated much more controversy than mine, had had his day on the Senate floor. Many other people were disappointed also; thousands of people had sent letters to the committee in support of my nomination, including the American Medical Association, the American College of Obstetricians and Gynecologists, Planned Parenthood, and others; the White House had received over six thousand supportive phone calls, and fewer than three thousand opposed. I will be forever grateful for that outpouring of support.

More than any other, the person most responsible for permanently stalling my confirmation vote was Senator Phil Gramm, and I regretted that I hadn't even met with him face-to-face. However, I did manage to have a very small pleasure at his expense. Months later, I happened to be in Orlando and a newspaper reporter asked me, "Dr. Foster, why do you think people tried to block your nomination?" I laughed and said, "Maybe you should talk to Phil Gramm, since he seems to have a lot of time on his hands just now." He had just dropped out of the presidential race, and I admit I wasn't sorry he'd made such a poor showing.

After the Senate failed to bring my nomination to a floor vote, President Clinton and I met. I told him I was disappointed, of course, but that I would be fine. I was eager to get back to my research and my life, which had been so disrupted during the nomination and hearing process. He congratulated me on how I had conducted myself, with dignity and forthrightness, and he told me he believed that I had much to contribute to the health care of the people of this country, and he wanted us to stay in touch. Senate vote notwithstanding, he thought I was the best person to deal with issues surrounding teen pregnancy, and he thought he would find a way to use my skills and expertise to some advantage.

The President invited me to play golf at a country club in Little Rock. If you really want to know something about a person, play a round of golf with him. It's an unusual game: you keep your own score, you have to call penalties on yourself. It's a game of honor, and you can learn quite a lot about your companions. I enjoyed my game with President Clinton very much, and it was clear to me that he is an extremely bright man of high integrity. I was confident that he would keep his word about finding a way to keep me engaged on a national level.

Six months later, as I was finishing up my sabbatical in Washington, the President invited me to be his Senior Advisor on Teen Pregnancy and Youth Issues. In this position, I would be an advocate for the lives of the young people I felt so committed to. Although I don't get paid, at least not in hard cash, I feel amply rewarded. I've found that this is the work I like to do best: travel around the country, help communities wrestle with the complex problems associated with the epidemic of teen pregnancy, and such closely related, really inextricably related issues of substance abuse, violence, poverty, crime, etc. As I have found so often in my life, my father's words came true; he had always told me not to worry about the future, that when one door closes, another one opens.

CHAPTER EIGHT

Common Sense and Determination

HEALTH CARE IN AMERICA

As Senior Advisor to the President for Teen Pregnancy and Youth Issues I speak to groups all over the country about subjects of medical and social concern. I tell people the facts, and the figures, and I tell people my story—what we were able to accomplish in Tuskegee and Nashville, with common sense and determination. When people are informed of the terrible inequities in our health-care system, and when they learn about how our system short-changes those very people it should be serving, they respond with compassion. Even better, my audiences often express a desire to help rectify these inequities. My mission, beyond anything else, is to ignite this determination.

Bringing healthy babies into the world has been the central focus of my work, and I passionately believe that the health of the nation's children should be a primary concern for everyone. But for children to be healthy, their mothers have to be in good health, even before conception takes place. And many American women are not in good health for a variety of reasons. Some because they have little access to adequate medical services, others because they are poor and unaware of the services that are available to them; others because they live in regions where there are no medical services; others because social and emotional factors impact on their well-being. Whatever the reasons, the entire country pays a high price for the health problems which affect our nation's girls and women—and, consequently, their children.

The statistics tell a terrible tale. As a nation, we are used to thinking of ourselves as superior to most others, but this is not true in the area of health care, and especially not in the health care of women and children. Although American women are living longer than ever before, their life expectancy ranks only sixteenth among industrialized nations. According to the Centers for Disease Control and Prevention, each year 6 million American women, half of them teenagers, acquire a sexually transmitted disease. As many as 20 million women are chronically infected with genital herpes or the human papilloma virus. Ectopic pregnancies quadrupled during the 1980s as a consequence of the increasing number of women with pelvic infections. A decade ago, AIDS was not even listed as a cause of death among women; in 1996, it was among the leading causes of death among women twenty-five to forty-four years of age. Clearly, action needs to be taken in order to turn these numbers around.

Girls and women are increasingly at risk for psychological disorders, which can have serious physical consequences as well. Cases of anorexia and bulimia have doubled over the past decade. Panic disorder strikes twice as many women as men. Depression, from mild to severe, is rife among girls and women. Even the medical community has been slow to recognize how intricately linked are emotional and physical symptoms and to develop appropriate interventions.

Another serious health hazard affecting many women is the appalling level of domestic violence in this country. More than a million women a year seek help for injuries caused by battering; and the number of battered women who never report their abuse is known to be much higher. These tragic figures represent only a small fraction of the situation, for we know that almost 90 percent of women who are physically abused by their spouses or partners don't talk, not even to their doctors—90 percent! We do know, however, that more than 1,300 women are murdered by their husbands or boyfriends each year.

These problems—medical, psychological, and social—produce drastic consequences when women, especially teenagers, become pregnant and have children. When children have children, which is to say when mothers are children themselves, their babies have many more health problems than when mothers are more mature.

In his 1995 State of the Union address, President Clinton identified teen pregnancy as one of the most significant problems facing the nation and he initiated a National Campaign to Prevent Teen Pregnancy in an attempt to wrestle with this issue. This program offers guidance and technical assistance to local communities so that they can better utilize the resources they have to reduce the incidence of teen pregnancy. Private and nonpartisan, led by former New Jersey governor Tom Kean, the goal of this program is to reduce the number of teen pregnancies by one-third by the year 2005.

No one expects easy or simple solutions to this complex issue; certainly the government recognizes that teenage pregnancy cannot be impacted with decrees and edicts from Washington. "Just say no" simply won't do the trick. Each locale—and there have been thirteen communities which have received CDC funds for this effort thus far—is charged with deciding the best way to use government resources. Whether business leaders are encouraged to donate computers to undeveloped neighborhoods or the amount of family life education in the school curriculum is increased or the community's males are targeted for education so that they become more responsible, each intervention is specific because local communities understand their own problems better than distant officials. We learned that in Nashville: ask the people what they need and then tailor the intervention program appropriately.

The President believes, as I do, that instilling a greater sense of personal responsibility in young people for the consequences of their behavior is the best long-term strategy for combating teen pregnancy. That means placing the first emphasis on abstinence.

At the same time teenagers must be provided with good reasons to remain abstinent; they must have opportunities for education and jobs, and some hope for their own futures. Ideally, this two-pronged strategy—responsibility and opportunity—will encourage young people to make better choices for themselves. The success of Nashville's I Have a Future program, and others like it throughout the country, illustrates that various initiatives can make a difference in the lives of our children.

But for such an effort to be successful, everyone has to become involved: parents, schools, civic leaders, business, religious organizations, health-care providers, government, and local communities. No one can sit back and hope that the next person will take some responsibility for the tragedy being played out in all of our neighborhoods. In Nashville, for example, it took only a handful of committed people to help a group of adolescents succeed when otherwise they might not have.

Although most people realize that teenage pregnancy is a problem, its magnitude is generally underappreciated. Here's more shocking information. Over a million teenage pregnancies will occur in this country this year, most of them unplanned; half this number, 500,000, will be intentionally aborted. And those babies born to single teenage mothers are at a tremendous disadvantage, even before they take their first breath. Research shows that children born to teens have lower cognitive development, are more likely than others to repeat a grade in school and to be victims of abuse and neglect. Eighty percent of children who were born to unwed teenage mothers who have not completed high school will live in poverty. By contrast, only 8 percent of children born to parents who are twenty years old and married, and are high school graduates, will live in poverty. Children born to teens are more likely to drop out of school, to divorce or separate, to themselves give birth out of wedlock, and to be dependent on welfare.

We have to ask ourselves what we are doing wrong, how we are failing our children. These statistics are not the result of inevitable circumstances, for other countries are much more successful than we are with these problems. In the United States, the annual teen pregnancy rate is 111 per 1,000 females aged nineteen and below, more than double that of the United Kingdom, next in line, which has 46 per 1,000. To put this in a more global context, the Netherlands and Japan have only 10 pregnancies per 1,000, making the situation in the United States 1,000 percent higher than in these other countries.

Why should this be? Some adults assume that the rise of teen pregnancy is the result of economic issues, that children become pregnant because of their deprived and impoverished environment. But the numbers reveal something quite different. Teenage pregnancy is not confined to poor minority children but cuts across all ethnic, economic, and social classes. If we consider only white teenagers who become pregnant, our relative statistical ranking in relation to other nations doesn't change at all.

Furthermore it is often assumed that the reason other Western nations have lower birth rates than the United States is that they have higher abortion rates. Not so. In fact, abortion rates in the United States are substantially higher than those for other Western nations. The United States ingloriously leads all other Western nations by a twofold margin in this category. In Sweden and France, teenagers become sexually active even earlier than do teenagers in our country, yet their pregnancy, birth, and abortion rates remain much lower than America's.

The causes of premature childbearing are multiple and extremely complex, and I don't pretend to be able to pull a solution to this destructive behavior out of a hat. Adolescence is a particularly tenuous time in a person's life, the period that spans the ever-widening gulf between childhood and adulthood, and the physical and emotional upheaval associated with this time is significant.

Adolescent girls in particular have an especially serious challenge because they are confronted with a biological/social paradox. A hundred years ago, the average age when girls began menstruating was around seventeen years old. Over the course of the twentieth century, this age has been dropping progressively: by six months every decade. Now the average age of menarche is just over twelve years old. Ironically, then, while biological maturity is occurring at an earlier age, it is doing so at a time when the complexity of our social structure actually requires a longer period of time to prepare for successful participation in it.

We must find a way, as a society, to help our youth enjoy and appreciate their adolescence rather than suffer through it. At the very least, we need to have trained professionals to specifically address the concerns of this age group, because adolescent problems are neither those of childhood or those of adulthood. The medical community itself comparatively recently recognized the unique needs of this group. The Society for Adolescent Medicine was founded in 1968; the American Medical Association recognized adolescent medicine as an area of specialization in 1977; and the American Academy of Pediatrics formed a section on adolescent health in 1978. It is clear that we need to make up for lost time and attempt to redress what our lack of vision has cost us.

Along with the physical factors which enable adolescents to become sexually active before they may be emotionally or psychologically prepared, our "open" society encourages sex by endorsing a glittering sexuality. The media stimulate and titillate our youth with sexual messages in every form—in music, lyrics, dance, dress, even food—from the very moment of awakening to retiring at night. Sex sells. Certainly there is no legal requirement that the media be socially responsible or that it illuminate the consequences of the type of behavior it glorifies. But then someone has to be responsible.

It would seem reasonable that the nation's educators would have the job of educating our youth, but tragically they are prevented from doing so by a small but very powerful conservative minority that believes that the dissemination of this information is dangerous, that teaching adolescents the important facts about their own reproductive health will increase sexual activity. This attitude is simply absurd and results in dangerous consequences, not the least of which is unwanted pregnancy, STDs and HIV/AIDS.

Teenagers are sexual. That is an uncontestable fact. And hoping the situation will change if we bury our collective heads in the sand or elsewhere is clearly foolish. The conspiracy of silence must end; our children deserve, really require, an honest and open communication about sexuality. But politics is tightly entangled with education, and blocks such dialogue. Look at what happened to former Surgeon General Joycelyn Elders when she suggested that masturbation, a natural and normal impulse, be openly discussed. The great hue and cry drummed her out of office.

If you ask the majority of Americans how they feel about sex and family life education, they are strongly in favor of it. Contrary to the claims of the conservative right, they realize that education doesn't mean promoting condom use but rather is about providing youngsters with the tools they need to build self-esteem and to help them avoid situations which might make them vulnerable.

Countries that offer comprehensive sex education and family life programs emphasizing abstinence and contraceptive services have the lowest rates of teen pregnancy. Although research shows that such programs are successful, many of our political leaders are more committed to avoiding controversy than to protecting the nation's children, and so there are few educational programs available to our young people. Except for the past three years, the United States is the only industrialized nation in the world where teen pregnancy and childbearing has increased in recent decades. Shame on us.

When we realize the consequences of failing to educate and inform, we have to ask ourselves: how is it that this small minority of ultraconservatives has so much influence over what our children can know? The answer is not especially complicated: many Americans don't vote. According to polls, only 37 percent of eligible Americans vote on a regular basis, barely one in three. But approximately 80 percent of the ultraconservative faction in this country vote, which is why their voice often rises over all the others and they can dictate the quality and quantity of the information which we teach our children.

Think of the numbers of people who have been ostracized, jailed, brutalized, and even murdered to attain and ensure this privilege; it seems like a sacrilege not to exercise it. If ninety-year-old women in South Africa can walk all day in 90-degree heat to cast their vote, we should be able to get into our air-conditioned cars to drive to the nearby polls. Nothing could be more important. Those who govern have responsibility, primarily, to those who have chosen them, which is why it is crucial that all the members of the society exercise the franchise.

Adolescents are not the only members of our society who desperately need to be educated. Part of the message which I have been carrying into local communities since becoming the President's Advisor is that adults need to overcome their discomfort with discussions of sexuality and openly communicate with their children. Someone will teach children about sex; who better than the adults who care about them? We have research which shows that 72 percent of boys and 63 percent of girls first learned about sex from someone other than their parents. The implications of these figures are far-reaching. When parents fail to teach children the facts about reproductive responsibility and their own values about sexuality, teenagers fail to learn how to manage the sexual situations they are bound to encounter.

Because children, parents, teachers, and health-care providers are not communicating openly and usefully about sexual issues, adolescents typically do not seek family planning until almost a year after the first act of intercourse. Adult silence and condemnation may lead to an unintended and unwanted pregnancy, and may result in an induced abortion. We are quick to shake our heads in dismay at the numbers of teenage pregnancies in our midst, as if we are not in some way culpable for the tragic lack of self-esteem which allows youngsters to give up hope for a rewarding future. Let's look to ourselves first, before we condemn our children and ask if we are really doing our job.

Those pregnancy prevention programs which are offered generally target girls, but this focus is inadequate. Men are every bit as responsible for a pregnancy as are girls, and need to be held accountable for their actions. Although this is obvious, society still seems to condone a "boys will be boys" attitude, that it is somehow normal and acceptable that young men "sow their wild oats." Now, we find that we are reaping what has been sown, and the entire society is faced with serious consequences. Boys need to be taught that they will be men only when they behave in a responsible way.

Adult men prey on young women. Two-thirds of teenage mothers are impregnated by men twenty years old and over. Men six or more years older than their female consorts cause more than 400 teen pregnancies *every single day!* Statutory rape laws, which generally define rape as males over eighteen having intercourse with females under eighteen, are not taken seriously or prosecuted in many states. More often than not, men who rape young girls simply walk away. Predatory men need to be included in counseling and education programs if teen pregnancy is to be reduced.

Male partners exert tremendous pressure on the young women they impregnate. In our I Have a Future program we stress the importance of male responsibility; our goal is to decrease the amount of coercion and violence used against women, and it has proved successful. When sex education programs focus on respect for females, the role of mutual consent in sexual encounters, and an awareness of the dangers of precocious sexual activity, they are offering the tools adolescents need to cope with difficult situations. A shocking 81 percent of American teenagers have been exposed to unwelcome sexual advances, and an even more shocking 60 percent of students in a recent study made an unwelcome sexual advance—believing that it was normal and appropriate behavior! Our kids have a great deal to learn and it is our responsibility to teach them.

Not just parents, or teachers, or government agencies—everyone has to be committed to protecting the nation's children. Americans are only beginning to confront the unspeakable level of sexual abuse of children in this country. Those children are among the most vulnerable in the society, especially sexually vulnerable. Many young girls who become pregnant, as many as 62 percent it has been found, are victims of past sexual abuse. Abused children may have trouble developing boundaries that enable them to resist older men who take advantage of their vulnerability. Research has shown that victims of early sexual abuse often feel powerless to affect events in their lives and suffer from low self-esteem. Even the notion of using contraception to prevent pregnancy is predicated on the belief that one's body is worth protecting, and many abuse victims don't possess this most basic instinct. This serious public health problem must be addressed by the judicial system, the legislative system, the federal and state governments, as well as by social service agencies and medical providers.

As terrible as the epidemic of teenage pregnancy is in this country, it is only one of the major health crises that the United States will have to address in the coming years. Before we can hope to have healthy adolescents, we need to ensure that our younger children have basic health services—which at present they do not. Although this country has the best health-care providers and facilities in the world, the health-care outcome for our own citizens is substandard in virtually every category when compared with other industrialized nations.

America's children are especially at risk. The United States ranks seventeenth, nineteenth, or twentieth in infant mortality for Western nations, depending on who's doing the counting. This appalling situation is the result of many factors, among them poor prenatal care, a lack of access to medical services, a failure of education, and a lack of social support.

And poverty. For many children, poverty is their main hazard. The poverty rate for children under six is nearly 60 percent in the United States—that is, 6 million children. It is unthinkable that this many children are living in poverty, but they are, and this terrible statistic should be unacceptable to every one of us. Children who are born poor, who live in urban slums or rural squalor, need our help, if for no other reason than that the consequences of hopelessness, social and medical, are profound and costly.

Children who live in poverty experience many more health problems than do children of families with adequate incomes, and rates of infant mortality and overall childhood mortality are higher among poor children. In addition, incidences of death by certain illnesses are higher: sudden infant death syndrome (SIDS), accidental injuries, child abuse, and infectious diseases, including AIDS. Poor children suffer disproportionately from low birth weight, asthma, measles, nutritional problems, dental decay, lead poisoning, learning disabilities, child abuse and neglect, and have higher rates of hospitalization than others.

Unstable or dangerous physical environments obviously compound the difficulties for poor children, especially children without permanent homes, children of parents who are migrant workers, and children in foster care. Native American children and children who live in poor rural areas also experience special health problems.

But economic status is only one indicator of increased health risks. There are significant disparities in the distribution of health care by ethnicity. For example, it is twice as likely for an African-American baby to be born under the normal birth weight, and the incidence of AIDS is much greater among black and Hispanic children than in other groups. Today, an infant born in Tobago, Trinidad, Jamaica, or Cuba has a better chance of surviving its first year of life than does a black baby born in America, the wealthiest nation in the history of humankind.

When a woman gets pregnant, insurance or not, she should have access to prenatal care. Of all the developed nations, believe it or not, only the United States and the Republic of South Africa fail to provide universal care for expectant mothers and babies. Comprehensive care is a feasible goal, if we are willing to provide it. The cost of providing every woman who needs it with access to prenatal care would be about the cost of two and a half stealth bombers ($1.9 billion). Given that there are about two dozen stealth bombers in our fleet at present, I think giving up the equivalent of two and a half of them for our nation's children is a small price to pay for healthy babies—even a wise investment. Our legislators have assisted other populations; they have lifted the elderly out of poverty while leaving many young families in dire circumstances. If every criminal in this country has a right to a lawyer, then certainly every sick child should have the right to a doctor.

Further, the lives of these babies need to be protected throughout childhood. Although we have laws designed specifically to enhance the health of the nation's children, more often than not, these laws are not seriously enforced. Take cigarettes, for example. It is a well-known fact that childhood tobacco use contributes to the ill health of millions of children. While virtually all states have laws prohibiting sales to individuals younger than eighteen, not one state adequately enforces its minimal age law. This failure contributes directly to the fact that more than 3,000 children in the United States start smoking every day, and this number is on the rise.

The Clinton Administration is attempting to respond to the urgency of this problem by proposing a comprehensive plan to reduce smoking among children and adolescents by 50 percent by the year 2000. The President has mandated that tobacco companies spend $150 million per year on anti-smoking education, but this amount may be insignificant compared with the $6 billion a year that the cigarette industry spends promoting smoking. The country has to rally behind the President if we are to curb the influence of these advertisements and save our children from preventable diseases, disability, and premature death.

According to the Centers for Disease Control, most illness in this country is related to tobacco use, sexual behavior, eating habits, sedentary lifestyle, misuses of alcohol and other drugs, and violent and abusive behavior. Clearly, medical intervention alone will not improve the health care of anyone suffering from health problems associated with a destructive lifestyle, but public health services can make a tremendous difference, and save the country enormous amounts of money.

Public health has frequently been overlooked as a resource because it relies, not on high-tech equipment and fancy space-age machinery, but on simple, commonsense solutions which serve everyone, regardless of age, gender, economic level, ethnicity, or geographic location. For example, mandated immunization and newborn screening programs, both public health initiatives, have reduced death and disability rates for children. Programs which provide easy and accessible high-quality prenatal care have contributed to reduced levels of low birth weight and lowered the rate of infant mortality. Public and community health services which have stressed injury prevention—such as improved vehicle design, use of car restraints, smoke detectors, fire-retardant clothing, childproof medicine caps, window barriers, lead-free paint, etc.— have led to a decline in the rate of childhood deaths and injuries.

Government funds set aside for public health services are used to protect the health of the community and can monitor hazards that would be impossible to screen otherwise. These funds work to maintain clean water supplies, examine meat for disease, and, most important, supply services to people who don't have health insurance. Public health clinics provide immunizations for children who might otherwise remain unvaccinated, and offer prenatal care for pregnant women.

More and more frequently in the past few years, public health agencies have been called upon to bolster our nation's inadequate healthcare delivery system, and this increase in responsibility has come at a time of chronic underfunding. We need to commit more resources to public health efforts. Although we spend millions of dollars developing miracle vaccines, an effort that is necessary and wonderful, we spend almost nothing to ensure that the end product gets distributed where it is most needed. In some cities, almost 40 percent of all children under two are incompletely immunized and thus left vulnerable to entirely manageable diseases. Where is the sense—or cents, for that matter—in that? Increasing public health services must be an integral component for the health paradigm for the twenty-first century.

With education and a commitment to public health, many of the health problems that seem overwhelming could be managed. We need a kind of domestic medical Marshall Plan, an effort similar to the one that was put forth to rebuild postwar Europe. We need to concentrate our health-care services where they are most needed. For example, the best facilities and physician-patient ratios should be located in the inner cities and rural areas of this country because that is where the need is greatest. That's just common sense, but at present it just doesn't happen.

Providing these regions with public health services is absolutely mandatory if we are going to improve the health-care situation for the inhabitants. Rural areas pose a particularly serious problem because so many people are involved; one-fourth of all Americans live in communities with fewer than 2,500 inhabitants—a total of 62 million people—so a dearth of services in these regions constitutes a major health problem.

There is a program in place which, if expanded, could bring medical services into these areas. The National Health Service Corps helps finance the medical education of qualified students if they are later willing to repay their "student loans" by working as medical personnel in underserved areas. Not only does the Corps address the issue of geographical workforce disparity but by offering scholarships and loans to people who may not have the resources for a medical education on their own, the program enables more minority students to become physicians.

Another commonsense solution which might bring services to those areas which need them most would be to create partnerships between Veterans Administration hospitals and rural communities. In Tuskegee, for example, two out of three hospitals have been forced to close due to financial problems, leaving many of its citizens without a medical facility. At the same time, the VA hospital in Tuskegee, built and sustained with public funds, has empty beds. Solutions are possible, especially if we make use of our existing resources.

The need for public health interventions will actually increase as health-care delivery systems change—and change they must. Currently our health-care system does not provide the best return for our investment, especially when compared with other nations. We now spend more than $2.5 billion a day for health-care expenditures and at our current rate of spending, this expenditure will exceed $1 trillion annually in just over two years—a quadruple increase since 1980. Health-care spending represents 14 percent of our gross domestic product (GDP); other advanced nations spend only about 6 percent of their GDP on health care, yet their coverage is universal and their health outcome is superior to ours in virtually every category.

Once again, we need to recognize how intricately related are politics and health services. An attempt at health-care reform legislation on a national level was introduced during the Truman Administration, but conservative politics prevented its passage. Then again, in 1965, the Johnson Administration introduced legislation to create Medicare and sought input from the American Medical Association, but the AMA characterized the program pejoratively as "socialized medicine" and refused to offer the required information. Ironically, the medical input necessary to craft the Medicare legislation was provided instead by the National Medical Association (NMA), an organization founded over a hundred years ago to provide an educational and political forum for physicians of color who had been systematically denied membership in the AMA. Now, some thirty years later, we again see the negative impact of politics on our attempts at health-care reform.

Changing the way we provide health care requires that we adjust the facilities and providers of those services. In a managed-care system, the wave of the future, according to a study commissioned by Congress, by the year 2000 there will be a shortage of 20,000 general practitioners and a surplus of 125,000 specialists. Despite this knowledge, most medical school graduates in this country entered the non-primary-care specialties.

It would make better sense to train physicians for what is needed. Therefore public funding should be used to encourage the delivery of a workforce which will meet the needs of the health-care system of the next century. Working with allied health professionals, nurse practitioners, certified nurse midwives, physician assistants, etc., to offer patients a variety of services is necessary to the future of our country's health care. Common sense dictates that we support that transition.

The challenges facing us in the coming millennium are daunting. We need to support health-care reform, even when that support entails changing our attitudes, and maybe even our politics. I consider it absolutely essential that the country hold its leadership responsible for doing its job in helping communities attack these problems. Thomas Jefferson told us over two hundred years ago that we must value health—that without health we have nothing. We haven't listened well.

As we exercise the vote, we need to think about policies and programs, rather than politicians. Those seeking our vote must bring with them policies that are in the best interests of our communities, especially the support of public health programs. We must become a political force that will ensure that those who are in agreement with our policies are the ones who are elected. I may sound biased here, but I look at the midterm elections of 1994 and I see a group of lawmakers whose programs and policies are anathema to our long-term survival. We cannot expect politicians to solve every problem, but we must see to it that people who care about the rights and concerns of everyone are elected to public office.

As I make my way around the country, talking to groups of concerned citizens, I find that most people want to help make a difference. President Calvin Coolidge offered what I think is the best observation on this I've ever heard:

> Nothing in this world can take the place of persistence. Talent will not; nothing is more common than unsuccessful men with talent. Genius will not; unrewarded genius is almost a proverb. Education will not; the world is full of educated derelicts. Persistence and determination are alone omnipotent. The slogan "press on" has solved and always will solve the problems of the human race.

Let us, as a nation press on.

Index